T0195888

PERSPECTIVE ON ANALYTICAL WRITING A FOCUS ON FEATURE AND EDITORIAL WRITING

RICHMOND S. ANDERSON, SNR.

authorHOUSE®

AuthorHouse™
1663 Liberty Drive
Bloomington, IN 47403
www.authorhouse.com
Phone: 833-262-8899

Published by AuthorHouse 12/06/2021

ISBN: 978-1-6655-4096-4 (sc)
ISBN: 978-1-6655-4094-0 (hc)
ISBN: 978-1-6655-4095-7 (e)

Library of Congress Control Number: 2021920794

Print information available on the last page.

This book is printed on acid-free paper.

APPRECIATION

The publisher with deep appreciation acknowledges the use of the following:

Excerpts from "An Anthology of Students Articles in Educational Administration", printed by the BEE Companies, Liberia. Excerpts from articles (editorial) from The Publisher Newspaper", Monday 16th – Tuesday 17th, April 2018, published by 3GH CONSULT, Ghana. Excerpts from articles (editorial) from "The Chronicle Newspaper", Friday 27th, April 2018, published by General Portfolio Limited, Ghana. Excerpts from articles (editorial) from "The Inquirer Newspaper", Tuesday 20th, January 2008, published by New Era Publications, Limited, Liberia.

AUTHOR'S PREFACE

The writing of this book, *Perspective on Analytical Writing a focus on Feature and Editorial writing,* is based on the urge for students majoring in mass communication on the African continent, particularly those within the Economic Community of West African States (ECOWAS), to have a simplistic understanding of the course **feature and editorial writing.**

It will be oblivious or a miss calculation to say that there are no texts books on feature and editorial writing on the African continent since I have not had the opportunity to extensively travel within Africa - but what could be safely said is, for over three decades since I completed my under graduate studies, I have not seen a text book on feature and editorial writing readily.

Based on this experience, the book first endeavored in its starting to give students an insight on what an *analytical writing* is, beginning with a drill on *perspective* and gave a detailed and vivid picture of perspective thereby laying the basis to understanding what *feature and editorial writing* is all about. Although the core focus of the book is on feature and editorial writing, but as the title depicts "Perspectives on Analytical Writing," more emphases are placed on perspective and analytical writing in order to provide a deeper understanding for the students as a foundation to grasp the concept of feature and editorial writing.

Also, the book featured research as a component to writing an appreciable feature and editorial piece. Added to research, other ingredients for writing good feature and editorials are also considered. They include *opinion, persuasion* and *propaganda*.

Furthermore, since feature and editorial writings are within the scope of mass communication and journalism, it became imperative for the book to touch on the ethical aspect of the profession aimed at providing students the barometer of knowing what to do and not what to do while writing feature and editorial pieces. In its conclusive stage, the book dealt with the impact of editorial on political actors as it relates to their involvement in the process of national development. As you will come across in your reading, mass communication and journalism are catalysts to agenda setting in any society - therefore, it is expected that stakeholders, particularly those involved in the governance process of our countries in Africa to take clue from editorial articles, especially those that advocate for positive change to propel them to respond to the developmental needs of Africa.

Now let's be practical and reflect on a simple analogy referencing a performance by a group of movie stars such as the late popular comedian, Peter Ballah of Liberia, Kekura Kamara with his popular movie "Malawala Balawala" of Liberia, Salla Kamara with his movie "Blood Diamond" of Sierra Leone, Mr. Ibu (John Okafor) with the show "Mr. Ebu and his son" of Nigeria or John Dumelo with the movie "the tie that binds" of Ghana. As these movie stars are performing in their movies, the viewers are fascinated with emotion, amusement and are thrilled by the performances while in their seats in the theatre, movie hall, or in their various homes. Just as the emotion of viewers is intrigued by the performances or movies, so feature and editorial write - ups are replica to evoking the emotion of the readers. The articles must create a scenario of curiosity to arouse or entice the readers. (**This is the drama in feature and editorial writing).**

ACKNOWLEDGEMENT

After several years of striving to have this book completed, it would not have been possible if other intellectuals and some individuals had not made their contributions for its finale. As stated in an African proverbial, "one finger cannot pick up lice", so is the case with the production of this book. I alone did not do it. In this regard, I take this opportunity to extend immense thanks and appreciation to the individuals mentioned bellow for their contributions in making it possible to arrive at my destination: This book will be incomplete if I don't pay homage to the Administration of the University of Liberia for giving me the privilege and opportunity to share my professional potentials at the university through teaching upon my graduation from the University of Liberia. Particularly, my profound appreciation goes to Rev. Dr. Professor J. Sarwolo Nelson, Jr. President of the University of Liberia for encouraging serenity and an ambiance of academic atmosphere for instructors and professors to demonstrate their intellectual potency through writing of academic materials or books which inspired me to do my debut writing of this book. Dr. Professor Moses M. Zinnah, Vice President for Academic Affairs, for his editorial inquest and encouragement to drive my appetite to remain focused in undertaking this project.

Thanks and appreciation is extended to Dr. Associate Professor Josephus M. Gray, Dean of the College of Social Sciences and Humanities, University of Liberia for enthusiastically embracing the idea when I informed him about the book project and his inspirational pep talks and cooperation exemplified.

Professor T. Nelson Williams, Sr. (demise) the founding Chairman of the Department of Mass Communication, University of Liberia for mentoring me into teaching through class presentations and his persistent encouragement for me to be studious in my quest to be a mass communicator. (Rest in peace Prof.).

The professional gladiator, Professor Weade Kobbah – Boley tutorage and encouragement lured me into writing. Her motivational and academic stimulationmade me to have published my first news story in a local daily as a student. That publication added to my professional zest to become an astute mass communicator.

(Thank you Prof.).

The eye opener, Professor Lamini A. Waritay, former Chairman of the Department of Mass Communication, University of Liberia taught and gave me the basic techniques for writing feature and editorial articles. His impartation gave me an eye opener and generated my interest in feature and editorial writing which is the nucleolus to the mass communication profession.

Dr. Professor Wingroove Dwamina, former Dean of the College of Liberal Arts and Humanities, University of Liberia for teaching me the basic steps of writing expository essays and his invite to join the university to serve as a Teaching Assistant after I graduated from the university. From that invitation, I gradually climbed the academic ladder to reach the rank of an Assistant Professor.

I will not also forget my longtime friend Rev. Professor J. Samuel Reeves for giving me meaningful guidance when he was informed about the project of writing this book. His encouragement contributed greatly to the success of the project. I also owe it greatly to my Bishop Isaac Kankam Boadue of the Grace Community Church International based in Kumasi, Ghana for taken me on a guided tour to the Palace of the Ashanti King to see and have historical insight of the Ashanti Kingdom, and to have also informed me about the movie industry of Ghana. Immense gratitude to my spiritual father, Pastor Owusu B. Randy, General Overseer of the Grace Community Church Liberia, for his many contributions toward the success of this book.

Great appreciation goes to Dr. John Gibson-Keykpo, Director of the Graduate School of Education at the state owned University of Liberia for editing and adding an internationally acclaimed academic flavor to the premier writing of this book. I will specially recognize veteran journalist and publisher of the Daily Observer Newspaper Kenneth Y, Best for taking up time to read the first draft of this book. Let me also remember the below listed persons including Sydney L. Nicol, Jr. of the University of Liberia for his little contribution to one of the case studies of the University of Liberia and James P. Anderson who served as "IT" technician for the book project.

DEDICATION

This book, "Perspective in Analytical Writing: a Focus on Feature and Editorial Writing" is dedicated to the youths of the global community with specificity on Africa, especially students within the Economic Community of West African States (ECOWAS), who are studying or aspiring to major in mass communication. You are the future shapers and agenda setters of Africa's information super high—way. Put your potentials and confidence into practice by analytically conveying the information of truth in your reportage through feature and editorial write-ups. It is also dedicated to my dearest loving wife Shirley G. Anderson (Mrs.) and the Andersons. You people are my courage and God my strength.

TABLE OF CONTENTS

CHAPTER ONE

PERSPECTIVE AND ANALYTICAL WRITING

As a student having a task to write an essay, if you take time to keenly examine your idea or subject you want to write on and read what others have written about it, then you might ponder so much as to whether you will not be able to cover your perspective sufficiently without turning your essay into a book. In such a situation you would have two options: briefly cover all the aspects of your idea or focus on a few key things.

If you preferred the first option, then your essay may seem too broad or general and it will be disjointed. Note that it is better to say a lot about a little rather than a little about a lot; as a writer always strive to cover too many ideas, you end up repeating the obvious as opposed to coming up with new intuitions. The second option leads to more interesting perspectives because you will focus on the most relevant parts of your idea or subject, allowing you to recognize undetected meaning that others might not have discovered.

To achieve your desired focus, you should take a second look at your main perspective or working assumption or thesis to see if you can narrow its scope. First consider whether you can concentrate on an important aspect of your idea or subject. For instance, if you were writing an essay on a health situation like COVID-19, look over your drafts to see which features keep coming up.

You might limit your essay to how the pandemic started, or, where it originated from, or, even better, the impact of COVID-19 on the world's economy, or better still, how many countries got affected from the pandemic, or yet still, how many people died from the menace of COVID-19 and how many people were economically affected?.

Next, see if you can delineate your perspective on the subject or idea more clearly, clarifying your argument or the issue you wish to explore. This will help you move from a "working" thesis, such as "The impact of COVID-19 on the world's economy". With this focus on the scope of your thesis, revise your essay to reflect just that. This will require you to engage in what is usually the most painful part of the writing process—editing or cutting. If something does not fit in with your perspective, it must be edited or cut off, no matter how tempting it may be.

NOW TAKE THE JOURNING TO ANALYTICAL WRITING

Understanding Perspective in Context

This aspect of the book is not intended to bore you with the rudiments of basic English; but as you are about to intellectually utilize same (book) leading your journey to the perspective on analytical writing within the framework of mass communication, particularly in feature and editorial writing, it is important to have a focal understanding of the word perspective as the basis to getting an insight of what to achieve from the book. In its simplistic term, perspective is the way you see something. If for instance you think that toy guns in Africa corrupt children's minds to think about war, then from your *perspective* a toy gun shop is an evil business center for African children - therefore, parents should not encourage their children to go to the toy gun shop – and parents themselves will not buy toy guns for their children.

Ainsworth (2005) notes that *perspective* is derived from a Latin word meaning "look through" or "perceive," all the meanings of *perspective* have something to do with looking. If you observe the world from a cat's perspective for instance, you will see through the cat's eyes. In drawing, perspective gives your drawing the appearance of depth or distance.

If we say someone "has perspective," we mean he or she has a sensible outlook on life. For instance, think about a way of thinking about something, especially one which is influenced by the type of person you are or by your experiences. This can be referred to as view point perspective. In any essay writing, perspective refers to writing where the writer gives his/her opinion that does not need to be supported, explained or documented.

This kind of a capstone paper Bernstein (1995) affirmed can be assigned to a topic which is specific, like as being instructed to write a perspective paper specifically on students' politics on campus. Your writing is told from the perspective of "you". Third person of view is used when your narration is not a character in the story. Unlike the assigned topic to give or write your view, writing an analytical piece from the perspective of a research oriented one, you have to go beyond just expressing your view (Bernstein, 1995). From Bernstein's proponent, it can be presumed that writing in perspective, your writing must be colorful by inserting imageries. This will instill in your readers an instant understanding of what you are trying to communicate or write.

What is Analytical Writing?

Before going into a dipper understanding on analytical writing, it is important to have some basic understanding on the etymology of the word analytical. Historical language such as linguistics, Achinein (1994) notes that the word analytical is derived from both Medieval Latin *analyticus*, and Greek *analytikus* which means "dissolved." With this etymological understanding, it can be briefly stated that analytical is the means of dissolving or breaking down of complex issues with smaller parts to find solutions.

Notwithstanding, analytical as a word is incomprehensible by an ordinary student who might have made a fair pass in freshman and sophomore English courses though the word might not be as difficult as it may appear. With this in mind, it is important to lay the basis for students to understand the word in its generality. Before dealing with analytical, a brief focus must be placed on two key words stated below:

Analyze and **Analysis.** Analyze as a verb is the process to separate into the constituent or parts, for the purpose of examining each part of the constituent separately. Do you understand this? This is the beginning of your critical thinking as you go through this book, it will make you be a good analyzer on issues if possible. Furthermore the drill of the book will broaden your knowledge on dealing with issues that readers will easily understand critically.

For your understanding, content knowledge generally refers to the facts, concepts, theories, and principles that are taught and learned in specific academic courses, rather than to related skills such as reading, writing, or researching which students also learn in school or university (Bernstein, 1995). Analytical writing is commonly required in academic writing, particularly in mass communication and journalism to show relationships between pieces of information. It is used to compare and contrast, assess or evaluate (for example, a number of approaches, theories, methodologies or outcomes on issue(s) under the spot light).

Analytical writing propels you to demonstrate your ability to articulate and support complex ideas, construct and evaluate arguments, and sustain a focused and coherent discussion at all levels. In analytical writing, it is always necessary to evaluate the issue you writing on, taking into consideration its complexities, and to develop an argument that includes reasons and examples supporting your views. A basic requirement for advanced essays at university level is that they are analytical. Analysis generally involves reorganizing information from the sources or data in order to make some relationship between the concepts.

The Four Major Types in Analytical Writing

Analytical writing is not only limited to mass communication or journalism. You can find such writing in English, philosophy, psychology or any other academic writing (Brande,1981).

The four types are:

- *Narrative Writing:* -Is a clear sequence of events that occur over time. Both what happens and the order in which the events occur are communicated to the reader. Effective narration of occurrence requires a writer to give a clear sequence of the events and to provide elaboration. This type of writing is mostly concern about telling a story where the writer tells a story about a real-life experience. If you were asked to write a narrative piece on the struggle and success/victory of the Ashanti people of Ghana when the British army fought hard to gain supremacy over them, you will have to do a thorough research in order to analytically write the real experience of the Ashanti Kingdom and its people, especially when you are not from within that segment of people to be a master of the information. In like manner, if you were asked to write on the settling of freed slaves from the Western World to the Shabro Island, Sierra Leone and their subsequent migration to the Providence Island located in Liberia in 1822 by a group of philanthropist, you will not give a clear narrative account if you do not conduct a research on the episode.

- *Descriptive Writing*: -This is the clear description of people, places, objects, or events using appropriate details. An effective description will contain sufficient and varied elaboration of details to communicate a sense of the subject being described. As the word implies, descriptive writing is a writing that depicts picture on issues you are writing about. For instance, if a group of mass communication students from within the African Sub–Region are invited to Ghana for site visit and one of the places to visit is the Palace of the Ashanti King in Kumasi and the students made a successful visit to the Palace. Upon their return to their respective countries and their mass communication instructors ask that they write an analytical piece from the tour made to Kumasi, regardless the students coming from different countries the fact remains, they will all write a vivid description of what they saw by giving a clear picture from their visit to the

King's Palace in Kumasi. The primary purpose for descriptive writing is to describe a person, place or thing in such a way that a picture is created in the reader's mind. Capturing an event through descriptive writing involves paying close attention to the details by using your entire five senses.

- *Expository writing*: -This type of writing that demands or seeks explanation, illumination or 'expose' (where the word 'expository' comes from). This of writing can include essays, newspaper, feature, editorial, and magazine articles, as well as other instructional write –ups as long as they seek to explain. The expository writing is a tool that is often used in academia. As a third year student of university majoring in any of the Liberal Arts courses (Mass Communication, English, Geography, French or any other liberal discipline), it is undisputable that you have written a paper/essay in either English course 410 or 421 (expository writing). Most expository essays have an introductory paragraph in which a thesis or objective is stated, several main body paragraphs that prove or explain what is in the introduction, and a concluding paragraph in which everything concerning your thought or issue is summed up. When writing an expository essay, it is important to write with the assumption that your audience or reader has little or no background knowledge about the main topic or idea. Your duty as the writer is to provide the reader with as much information as you can. The reader should feel as if he or she has learned something after reading your article.

- *Persuasive Writing*: -This is the writing that presents reasons and examples to influence action or thought of the reader. Effective persuasive writing requires a writer to state clearly an opinion and to supply reasons and specific examples that support his or her opinion. Your writing must convince your readers to prompt them understand your idea or communication. For example, if you want to write on an alleged huddle in the free movement within the African Sub - Region, and as an Information Officer assigned to the Regional Office responsible for the dissemination of information on activities of the office concerning the Region, you have the task to write a convincing piece that will alley any fear in the minds of the citizens within the African Sub-Region (that is persuasion).

Things to Know in Analytical Writing

An analytical writing is a piece that is written to achieve exactly what it implies, to analyze. When writing an analytical piece there are certain things you need to be familiar with, as listed below:

- You can choose any topic, but it is important to remember that the main aim of analytical writing is to give the reader a better understanding of the subject matter.
- Take the issue or subject you are writing about and separating the different categories within that subject. You should always know that in writing, there is only an issue to deal with in your piece or article. For instance, if your issue is the shortage of drinking water in the city, if even there are other problems that warrant residents to know about, your issue to concentrate on is that of the water shortage. (Deal with issues one at a time). *This is perfect communication.*
- In dealing with an issue break it down in categories, with a thorough analysis of each part. Example, if you were writing about a person, present your analysis based on examination of different stages of their life. In this case, the topics to examine would be childhood, marriage, career, education, and other things about the person. You would then examine the historical context of each category. With the example of writing about a person, analyzing the stages of their life will help the reader understand how that person's life progressed over the years. Each time you break down one of the topics in your essay, the information you provide helps to show the relationship between each of those sub topics, thus leading to a clearer understanding of the entire subject matter you are dealing with.
- Say you were researching a certain breed of animal, like a cat. You could research the ancestry of that breed and how it came

into existence. By following the history of the breed of the cat, you will discover how it came to have certain traits and characteristics because of its relation to other breeds. You would also be able to better understand why some cats have better behavioral skills, like the skill to kill rats in some homes, than others. When writing an article that requires research, usually your goal is simply to take one aspect of a topic and create your paper with a certain focus in mind, but with an analytical writing your goal is to look at all the different aspects of that particular topic or issue.

- Analytical writings are written so you can better understand how all those different issues fit together, giving your readers a complete understanding of the entirety of a subject matter or issue.

- In writing analytically, try not to rush your paper, take your time to analyze each part of the issues, point by point. You should know that this is an analytical paper, so the most important thing to remember is that you are striving to create an understanding, an explanation, of a certain topic or idea for your readers to understand you. If you make your issue or topic clear, and take the time to show the relationships between each category, then you should have the tools for a successful analytical writing.

Understanding Descriptive, Analytical, Persuasive and Critical Writing

The simplest type of academic writing is **descriptive**, and its purpose is to provide facts or information. An example would be a summary of an article or a report of the results of a laboratory experiment. However, it is rare for a university-level text to be purely descriptive. Most academic writings are also analytical. **Analytical** writing includes descriptive writing (i.e. facts or information), *plus* the added feature of *re-organization*. That is, in analytical writing you are not only giving information, but you also re-organize the information into *categories, groups, parts, types or relationships*.

Sometimes, these are categories or relationships which are already part of the discipline (e.g. in the discipline of Law, there are two types of law: common law and statute law). Sometimes, these are categories or relationships which you create specifically for your piece. (e.g. If you are comparing two theories, you might break your comparison into three parts, based on three aspects of the theories, such as: how each theory deals with social context, how each theory deals with language learning, and how each theory can be used in practice, for instance, the experiment of osmosis, can you still remember this from your biology laboratory?.

In most academic writings especially mass communication, you are required to go at least one step further than analytical writing, to that of persuasive writing. **Persuasive** writing has all the features of analytical writing (i.e. information, plus re-organization of the information) as well as the added feature of your own point of view.

Your point of view may be, for example, an interpretation of the findings, an argument or some recommendations. Most writings are persuasive -- and there are persuasive elements in least the discussion and conclusion of a research article. In persuasive writing, each claim that you make needs to be supported by some evidence – e.g. by a reference to an authoritative information that has been published. The kinds of instructions for a persuasive assignment could be, for example, argue, evaluate, discuss, and take a position.

Critical writing is usually common for research work in university writings. Critical writing has all the features of persuasive writing (i.e. facts plus re-organized, plus your point of view), with the added feature of at least one *other* point of view. That is, while persuasive writing requires you to have your own point of view on an issue or topic, critical writing requires you to consider at least two points of view, including your own. For example, you may explain a researcher's interpretation or argument, and then evaluate the merits and demerits of the researcher's argument, or give your own alternative interpretation. Most academic articles that you will write must have some parts which are more analytical or descriptive, and other parts which are persuasive or critical.

Developing a framework for Analytical Writing

Many students find it useful to develop an analytical framework or taxonomy which represents the way pieces of information have been grouped and related to others. There are many different ways of structuring information and ideas that are to be included in an essay or article. Brow (1999) notes that the structure that you set up might be a reflection of the way these ideas or issues are structured in the real world.

For example, the way one thing happens after another in a time sequence might not give you the relativity of what you actually want to know. If not, the structure might be based on your own interpretation of the real world-- for example, the way you think one thing is more important than another, or you are thinking about how to pay your tuition for second semester, and how to get a car upon completing your study at the university. Which of the two is more important ? Is it the tuition or the car? (Think it over).

Analytical frameworks involve abstract concepts as the basis for any analytical writing. Below are some common abstract frameworks for consideration:

--Advantages and disadvantages
--Issues or problems
--Factors, causes or reasons
--Consequences

These frameworks can help you in organizing your ideas in your writing and move to the detailed planning stage of your article preparation.

What is an Academic Writing?

In his learning Brande(1981) asserts an academic writing universally refers to a style of expression that writers and researchers use to define the intellectual boundaries of their disciplines and their specific areas of expertise such as mass communication. Characteristics of academic writing include a formal tone which is the use of the third-person rather than first-person perspective (usually) -- a clear focus on the issue or idea you are dealing with for your message to be understood – and the use of precise choice of words. Throwing light on the stylistic writing elements, Brande(1981) noted that those academic articles in the social sciences including mass communication can vary considerably depending on your writing style and the intended target and audience. However, most university-oriented papers require meticulous attention to the below stylistic elements:

> *Looking at the bigger picture* – Unlike fiction or other professional writing, the overall structure of academic writing is formal and logical. It must be cohesive and possess a logically organized flow of ideas. This means the various parts are connected in order to form a unified whole. The narrative in your writing should link the sentences and paragraphs so as to enable the reader to follow your thoughts. The introduction should include a description of how the rest of the paper is organized.

> *The Tone of your Writing* - The overall tone for this book refers to the attitude conveyed in a piece of writing. Throughout your article, it is important that you present the arguments of others fairly and with an appropriate narrative tone. When presenting a position or argument that you disagree with, describe this argument accurately and without such being loaded with biased language (Brande, 1981). Drawing from Brande (1981) accession, let it be noted that in analytical writing, the writer is expected to investigate the issue from an authoritative point of view. You should, therefore, state the strength of your arguments confidently; using language that is neutral—and not being confrontational or dismissive.

> *Diction* - Diction in this case is the choice of words you use in your writing or article. Awareness of the words you use is important because words that have almost the same denotation (dictionary definition) can have very different connotations (implied meanings). This is particularly true in analytical or other scholastic writing because words and terminology can evolve a nuanced meaning that describes a particular issue,

idea, concept, or phenomenon derived from the epistemological culture of what you are writing about at the time. In this connection, use concrete words that will convey a specific meaning to your readers or audience.

> *Be Cautious of the Language you write* - The inquiry of an issue or idea you write analytically in the social sciences is often complex and multi-dimensional. Therefore, it is important that you use unambiguous language. Well-structured paragraphs and clear topic sentences enable a reader to follow your line of thinking without difficulty. Your language should be concise, formal, and should be expressed precisely to portray the actual meaning.

> *Observing your Punctuation* - Scholars all over the globe rely on precise words and language to establish the narrative tone of their work--therefore, punctuation marks are used very deliberately. For example, exclamation points are rarely used to express a heightened tone because it can come across as unsophisticated or over-excited.

> *Ability to have Higher-order Thinking* - Most analytical writing addresses complex issues that require high-order thinking skills to comprehend. Think of your writing this way: One of the most important attributes of a good teacher is the ability to explain complex ideas in a way that is understandable and relatable to the topic being presented. This is also one of the main functions of analytical writing which is aimed at describing and explaining the significance of complex ideas as clearly as possible (Brande, 1981).

How to improve your Analytical Writing?

To improve your analytical writing, there are three major areas you need to consider. They are:

❖ Your writing must be clear - The act of thinking about precedes the process of writing about. Good writers spend sufficient time distilling information and reviewing major points from the literature they have reviewed before creating their work. Writing detailed outlines can help you clearly organize your thoughts. Effective analytical writing begins

❖ *Consistent Stylistic Approach* -Regardless of the number of styles characterized or required in writing your paper or article such as MLA, APA or the *Chicago Manual of Style*, you should always choose one style manual and stick to it. Each of these style manuals provide rules on how to write out numbers, references, citations, footnotes, and lists. Consistent adherence to a style of writing helps with the narrative flow of your article and improves its readability (Richard, 2003).

CHAPTER TWO

FEATURE WRITING

THE NEWS MEDIA AS AN informational tool aims at achieving any entity's communication goals. One useful tool or writing material to realize this is a feature piece or article. Feature articles are more in-depth than the straight forward or traditional news stories and go beyond providing intriguing and important facts that are consumable. The purpose for feature article is to provide a detailed description of a person, people, a place, idea, or entity.

Many a time, most reporters and editors classify feature pieces as news stories, but in reality, they are not necessarily structured that way because they are not using the inverted pyramid style. Rather, feature articles use storytelling devices to help the reader or audience connect with the overall narrative and its central characters. Features are particularly common in professional dailies/newspapers or magazine writing, although they frequently appear in other media.

As a feature writer, it is always good to understand the circumstances that necessitate a feature article from a strategic communication point of view. Communication experts write consumable feature articles to provide in-depth exposure for their readers/audience or organization. This is where you exhibit the highest traits of understanding the issue.

If you want to urgently reach your readers or audience or entity to the media, a feature piece may not be the best tool to use due to is its detailed and lengthiness than a straightforward or a traditional news story. However, you could write a feature article on, for example, a company's new General Manager to provide more detailed and background information to targeted audiences. Feature stories can also be used in an entity's internal communication system such as, magazines and newsletters.

Most of the time journalists and feature writers often use news stories and feature articles interchangeably with the notion of both having the same meaning. However, feature articles are intrinsically different from news stories. While it is at times difficult to dichotomize between straight or traditional news and feature story, the differences sustain by and large under the general circumstances. With this understanding, Let us see what a feature story is in subsequent topic.

Definition

Feature by definition is a newspaper, magazine, or radio article or report of a person, event, an aspect of a major event, or the like, often having a personal slant and written in an individual style. Understand that a feature story is a type of soft news. The main sub-types are the news feature and the human-interest story. A feature story is distinguished from other types of non-fiction by the quality of the writing. Stories should be memorable for their reporting, crafting, creativity, and economy of expression.

A feature article Mencher (1998) notes is much more than a collection of barefacts. It's a special-interest article abounding with details that makes for pleasurable reading. While a hard news article focuses on exactly what happened, when and to whom, a feature article typically adds a dimension of human interest.

For Felder (2000), a feature is a special story or article written in a creative manner, sometimes subjective article designed primarily to entertain and inform readers of an event, a situation or an aspect of life in newspaper, magazine or at times radio. It shows human interest rather than straight news. The feature article gives information of human interest.

In his aversion Felder (2000) the label feature covers a broad range of newspaper or magazine articles which includes everything except straight news, editorials, or advertising. Due to its human-interest approach, the feature article, allows the writer considerable opportunity for creativity. While the subject of a feature may be related to a news item, the article will not follow a pyramid structure of a straight news piece. Rather, it is more likely to include conventions of fiction: plot, character, dialogue, and symbolism.

A feature is a creative article that deals with real events, issues, and trends; but unlike straight news articles, feature places emphasis on the people involved rather than on the facts of news. In its nature, a feature is a component or a course in mass communication that deals with unusual aspect of a news story or event, yet still, it is a news story written informally, providing information, education and sometimes entertainment depending on the issue or subject matter you are dealing with. Putting it in perspective, feature is an analytical writing with critical dimension that tends to evoke the curiosity or emotion of the readers.

Let it be also understood that a feature story is a type of soft news. The main sub-types are the news feature and the human-interest story. A feature story is distinguished from other types of non-fiction by the quality of the writing. Stories should be memorable for their reporting, crafting, creativity, and economy of expression. Equally so, a news feature is a kind of story that focuses on a hard-news topic. News features combine a feature writing style with hard-news reporting.

A feature story is any piece of writing that falls between the cut-and-dried news stories on one hand, and the w holly fictionalized story or opinionated essay on the other hand. It is the product of factual reporting and reporting to which are added story elements of imaginative writing and interpretation. The special feature article is similar to news story in that it gives the readers facts in an interesting form. But it goes beyond those facts by multiplying them with study, research, and interviews to instruct, and entertain the readers who know about the subject as well as those who do not know.

Feature stories can be news stories. Features can be investigative. Features can be in-depth studies. Features can be for fun. The subject can be anything: places- a community, a farm, a business, topics- education, science, economy, religion, philosophy; events-parades, programs, concerts; people-well known or unknown animals-unusual or ordinary; objects-art or product. In other words, features can be any subject of interest to society or the reader.

In his view McKinney (1986) a feature is an article beyond the realm of the straight or traditional news story's basic and unvarnished "5 Ws" and one "H". Furthering, McKinney (1986) states that the "justification, strength and the very identity of the feature article lies in its presentation of the imagination not however, in departing from or stretching the truth, but in piecing the peculiar and particular truth that strike people's emotion, sympathy, skepticism, humor, consternation or amazement".

Contextualizing McKinney (1986) accession, he is projecting that feature article is quite different from that of a straightforward or traditional news story. In straightforward or traditional news reporting, the writer is concerned about what happened, where it happened, why it happened, who is involved in the event and how it happened. Unlike the straightforward news, feature article goes beyond just the mere facts.

Feature article seeks to arouse or evoke the readers' interest or attention. For instance, if we were to draw the attention of readers to someone who from a least expected village gains prominence and you want to write a feature through profiling them, how would you begin your article to actually captivate the interest of your reader(s)? In short, a feature is a creative article that informs, explains, interprets, analyzes and exposes issues for the understanding of readers.

Pitching the media can be tough. Every day, reporters are inundated with breaking news from different sources, all clamoring for attention. One way to break through the cacophony is to offer a different type of article--one that speaks to a topic that is of interest to a target audience but not dependent on being newsworthy right at the moment it is sent. That type of article is called a feature.

A feature is an in-depth look at a topic, product or industry. It is a complex story designed to be read at a leisurely pace. And a feature can benefit any company by linking the brand or product to a larger trend or industry focus while also showcasing the entrepreneur, as a thought-leader in field of great competition. While a news release is designed to entice the reporters into finding out more information themselves, a feature is designed to be used as is, or merely edited to fit the space available.

Topics such as health, agriculture, gender issues, travel and technology all lend themselves well to feature articles since they can be used in special sections of newspapers. Trade publications also publish feature articles, usually in the form of special supplements. Because a feature should be written from a journalistic approach, you should emphasize information over outright promotion. Ideally, a feature editor will not change the story at all and will use it when it is needed as part of a theme or to fill space. Papers like to have quality articles on hand, so come up with your feature-worthy concept, and then use the following guidelines to help you write a great article.

See the below introduction as *an* example of a personality feature and determine whether you can grasp the idea or be on course. Do not border about the type of the feature (Personality profile) in subsequent reading you will come across same; this is just a tip of the ice box.

Example: (just an introduction) *According to the famous English writer, William Shakespeare of Great Britain, in one of his publications said "some men are born great, some achieve greatness and some have greatness trust upon them", such is the case with Sayou Youtay Anderson who was born in a little disadvantaged village where there was not even the least educational facility, is today one of the prominent personalities in the country.* (Can you attempt to complete the profile on Sayou Youtay Anderson by writing an imaginary piece of at least fifteen paragraphs?)

What is a Feature Story?

To put it in context, a feature article is a newspaper or magazine article or story that goes in depth with a particular topic or issue. In furtherance, a feature article a special story published in a newspaper or magazine, or a part of a television or radio broadcast that deals with a particular issue or subject categorized in a special manner under the nomenclature "special feature". In very simple language, feature articles lay more emphasize on people, places and events or issues that affect the lives of readers particularly.

Let us take a very simple example. A story that narrates the plight of the homeless people in Ganta, (Liberia) can be a feature story. While it is as important as a news story, it is not governed by the immediacy factor. Nonetheless, a news event can also inspire a feature story. While the news story will mainly focus on facts and figures and unveil the "5Ws" and "1H", the feature article will take a specific angle and go in-depth into the story.

A feature story is not really a straight or hard piece of news and is distinguished by the way it is written depending on the issue and the writer. In reality, feature stories should be unique in their style of reporting and should have a different style or way of writing and expression of the issue(s). It must be noted that a distinct difference between a hard or straight news articles and feature stories is, news is written with a direct rule to follow the inverted pyramid structure whereas, feature articles go by the upright pyramid structure.

To be more pragmatic, a feature must conform to the three-act structure of storytelling wherein the narrative is divided into three distinct compartments – the setup, the confrontation, and the resolution. Although this book is not for Political Science students, but it is important as a mass communicator, particularly feature writer(s) to be knowledgeable of how political speeches used by political actors are aimed at influencing their audiences. This is all intended for people to take positive action.

On this basis, the book wants to reflect your memories as far back to 1981 when David Steel of the Labral Party in Great Britain delivered a speech in 1981 at a conference that brought both the Liberal Party and the Social Democratic Party together. If you really followed the conference, you would have realized that at the time of Steel's address, inflation was at its highest peak in Britain, public unemployment was in the increase since 1930, public expenditure was declining, and there was instability in the inner cities of London, Liverpool, and Manchester.

In that conference, Steel identified four major tasks for the next government to handle, the first of which was industrial reconstruction to boost productivity in Britain. The second task was the third was constitutional reform founded on the principle of open and democratic self-government. The third was social reconciliation to build community relations. The final task was to increase Britain's influence abroad, particularly in Europe. That meeting was persuasive not because of the eloquence of the speaker, but the technique employed in his speech.

As we discuss the auxiliaries of feature, it is important we understand something known as the APPLAUSE Formula which a feature writer should subscribe to. APPLAUSE is the acronym for (Appeal, Plan Facts, Personalities, Logic, Action, Universal, Significance and Enthusiasm). Let us see how each of the above effectuate their importance in your feature article.

Appeal: Your feature article must arouse the interest of the reader(s). If it falls short of this, it cannot become a feature story. Your aim of the feature story is appeal to the senses of the readers. The global pandemic of Covid -19 appeals to the emotive chord of the readers and therefore it is potential feature material for most of the news organizations globally.

Plain Facts: As a feature writer, you must have the conviction that facts are stronger than fiction. There is an adage that says, if we are to believe this, it is obvious that facts sell more than fictions do. It means that if a feature report is to be accepted it must essentially deal with facts and not fiction. A reported feature must ensure that the feature has enough plain facts.

Personalities: If a feature story narrates the personal story of an individual who is important like celebrities, readers will be interested or lap it up. If we can take the example of the world most celebrated footballer Messi's recent interview in France published in any newspaper or a news magazine, copies of the concerned newspaper or news magazine will automatically be sold in quantity.

Logic: Indisputably, a feature story must conform to logical considerations. If it is not dictated by a natural flow of facts, the readers will buy the argument inherent in the story. The feature story must move from one part of the subject it is dealing with to the other part seamlessly. Let us take an example. If a story talks about the protest of the Council of Patriots held in Monrovia in 2019, it must start from how it was organized flow seamlessly into an account of the protests that happened. If the feature story deliberates only on the protests without taking into consideration the background, the story will remain logically incomplete.

Action: A feature article should ideally move readers into action. Only then, it fulfills its objective. What is journalism or feature writing if it does not gad readers into doing something? The inherent purpose of journalism is to bring about a positive change and a feature is a distinct tool to do just that.

Universal: A feature story should have an unquestionably universal orientation. It needs to be appealing and useful to every reader and sundry. At the same time, the feature story can do extremely well if it deals with something that is unique and essentially different.

Significance: Your feature article must ideally deal with a subject matter that has impact on people's lives. In short, the feature should have some relevance in the daily lives of people and society. Let us take an example. The increment of tariffs the government placed on GSM Companies in 2020 there by reducing the credits of the service consumers has a direct repercussion on the economic lives of Liberians.

Enthusiasm: A feature story should be assertive or emphatic in its approach. It should be convinced about its own subject matter. In other words, a feature story needs to be enthusiastic in nature.

Feature Article in its Generality

In its generality, you can write a good and acceptable feature piece if you consider the below listed feature article;

- Evokes an emotional reaction: Either joy, sympathy, anger, frustration or contentment.
- Gives in-depth and meaning to complicated issues or ideas, thus clarifying and interpreting events.

- Follows the techniques of creative writing; for example short story elements.
- Lacks the pyramid structure of a straight news story.
- Uses an introduction(lead) that attracts readers.
- Ends with a closing that connects back to the beginning and leaves the reader with something to remember.
- Uses a tone and style appropriate to its subject.
- Uses catchy titles, headings/subheads.
- Is a well-researched piece.

Feature Stories Versus an Opinion Piece

Feature article differs from the straight short story or soft news because it is factual and not fictional. Feature writers may, however use the devices of the short story, especially in narrative features, and they can feel justifiably proud if they are told that their feature article "reads like a short story". Feature differs from editorials, reviews, commentaries, and most columns in their approach to opinion. It is the difference between making reasonable judgment and advocating.

It is important for feature writers to note that they do not judge in their writing and should not advocate. They aim not at persuading as in the case of public relations, but at illuminating through creating imageries that would draw the attention of the readers. Some opinion pieces, notably columns by most movie reporters consist of interview features.

It is, however, dangerous for beginning feature writers not to recognize the subtle differences between features and most opinion pieces. Feature writers never attempt to persuade, they inform, educate and entertain readers through their critical and analytical posture or writing. As the word implies, opinion is expressing your own view on a discussed issue or matter, that is, how you feel about an issue.

Feature Stories Versus News Reports

Feature stories versus news reports will begin with an understanding of the differences in how feature writers or journalists approach both the reporting and writing of features. In news gathering and reporting, for instance, reporters give the recounting of factual and timely events to enable readers to cope with themselves and their environment. News is greatly influenced by events and determinants such as; timeliness, proximity, oddities, prominence, consequences and human interest. Reporters are under professional obligation to quote sources and make attributions. In feature stories/writing, the writer describes characters; create coloration and sometimes capturing their interaction through dialogue instead of through disembodied quotes.

There are other differences between the traditional news stories. According to Fry (1996), feature is the usage of what he termed as "gold coins". Explaining further, Fry (1996) noted that "gold coins" are those shinny nuggets of information on passages within feature stories that keep readers reading, even though the sections are based on weighty materials. The author also noted that a "gold coin" can be something as simple as a carefully selected detailed that surprises or charms, or it can be an interior vignette—that is, a small story within a larger story that gives the reader a sense of place or re-engages the reader in the story's characters (Fry, 1996).

Analytically, putting Fry (1996) professional proponent in context, feature article differs from that of the straightforward or traditional news story in many aspects. There is no standard form or a strait jacket for feature writing; the middle and the end should be as compelling as the beginning or introduction. However, feature writers should not ignore the hallmark of good news writing. Simplicity is as important in feature writing as it is in most news writing; but the tense statement of fact characteristic of the informative news story is seldom useful in feature writing. There is nothing else but the fact on the issue/idea you writing on.

Feature writers must always think of their writing as thematic, that is, what is the issue/idea you writing with the sentences and paragraphs tied to each other in such a way that a unified, coherent flowing story is produced or written. Although many feature stories are quite as timely as news stories, feature writers must not depend on timeliness for readers' interest. The single presentation of facts growing out of recent events is not for them (readers). Instead, the facts they use must be informed in color and life, background and not interpretation, imaginative perceptions of people and situations, and sharp bright phrases.

The writing styles of a news story and a feature are different. In a news story, the emphasis is on content rather than form. News stories go straight to the point, using simple and effective words to deliver the facts quickly.

The entire story usually average between 200-400 words depending on the issue you are reporting on. Some notion of the different flavor of features is apparent in the difference between most news leads and feature introduction (leads).

Below are examples of a straightforward news lead and an introduction feature story.

(a) *Many people today fled from the capital city for the interior as a result of intensive heat because of the dry season. (Straightforward news).*

(b) *As the country begins to experience the dry season coupled with acute shortage of drinking water, people of all class, notwithstanding the intensity of the heat, have find pleasure and for comfort to change temporal location from the capital to the interior part of the country (feature intro/lead).*

Exercise:

Examine both leads and state what made them similar or different. Develop similar leads on your own and write an imaginary news story on any current issue/event (six paragraphs) and an imaginary feature article on any contemporary issue (fifteen paragraphs).

Given a feature's propensity to apply the craft of showing rather than merely telling, feature writers need to develop and expand their reporting skill set. As feature writer, you need to become keen observer and listener rather than talker in order to boil down what you observe to what really is of relevance or matters not forgetting to deal with the issues, and to best describe not for description's sake but to move the article or story forward. This is a means to use all the effort to build a tight, forceful scene taking both practice and restraint. It is not compulsory to record everything that is seen, heard or smelled. If you do this as a feature writer, you will be overwriting and it will serve as a neon exit sign to most of the readers. All you do is to deal with the issues or ideas.

Another aspect that has to do with feature stories versus news reports is, writing as a continuum begins with the inception of an idea and making writing a consistent interrelated process. Just to share a professional experience with you, before going out on the field to gather information, as a reporter or feature writer, you should consider the range of your story; its central message or idea, the approach that appears to best fit the story or feature and even the tone you should take as a feature writer. Such forethought defines not only how a story will be reported and written but the scope of both. Framing and focusing early allows a reporter or writer to report or write less broadly and more deeply and further, assure authoritative story as well as reporting.

Before a feature writer can capture telling details and create scenes in their feature stories, they need to get these details and scenes in their notebooks. As stated earlier, feature writers need to be keen observers of the innocuous. In reporting stories, journalists, especially feature writers, generally gather specific facts and elucidating quotes from sources. Rarely, however, do they paint a picture of place, or take the time to explore the emotions, the motives and the events that led up to the news.

In summation, the chapter will conclude by leaving you with four basic but important areas that will easily refresh your memory on the subject matter that is, feature versus news report or story.

The areas are:

Content – In feature writing, any event or issue could be news-related or be of human interest whereas news writing or reporting, the events are news breaking news or recent occurrences.

Introduction – The introduction of a feature story often has a human focus or gives short account of events or anecdote. In news story, the introduction always summarizes the story in a nutshell.

Source and angle – The article of a feature piece always contains a variety of sources and angles. For news story or report, seldomly, but the event does not always contain more than one source and angle.

Structure – Feature story is more flexible and can take a linear or a non-linear structure including a story-telling conclusion, and in news writing the structure takes the inverted pyramid posture.

The News Feature

A news feature according to my learning, is a story that focuses on a hard-news topics which often combine a feature writing style with hard-news reporting. A human-interest focus on breaking news results in a news feature, an article which adds personal involvement to what may otherwise be a distant, seemingly unimportant current event. An interview with the parents of a soldier wounded in an overseas battle brings personal emotion into the report of an event in which readers may have no other involvement.

Writing Feature and News

Mass Media is a conglomerate of all media outlets and functionaries that include feature writing. Hence, writing for the mass media begins with learning how to write news. In this regard, this section of the book will endeavor to expose readers, especially students to the basic forms and some conventions of writing feature stories and news stories for the media.

In the media, particularly in the area of journalistic writing, the style of writing a formal, structured and demanding articles or stories is cardinal. The presentation of information not divorced from accurate information in an accurate context is the main goal of writing, rather than just presenting and developing an individual writer's style. No matter what kind of media outlet you want to use, all media writing attempt to present information accurately, clearly, efficiently and precisely. Meeting up with these goals are the major things involved in learning to write for the media, especially for technical writing such as feature and editorial.

With conventional writing, there are two important elements to always strive to know. They are attribution and modesty. For your understanding, attribution is informing or telling your readers or audiences the source(s) of your story or information--that is, where you got your information from. For modesty, you the writer attempt to stay within the confines or background of the report. (Do not put yourself in the story; leave it for the readers to make a determination on your news story)

Like in news reporting, feature stories are built from facts. Nothing in them is made up or embellished. In features, the facts are embedded in or interwoven with scenes and small stories that show rather than simply tell the information that is conveyed. Features are grounded in time, place, and in characters that inhabit both. Often, feature stories are framed by the specific experiences of those who drive the news or those who are affected by it. They are no less precise than news. They are less formal and dispassionate in their structure and delivery.

Note that feature writing centers mostly on people and interests rather than events, but many of the same writing conventions of news writing are also required for feature writing. It is important to understand that feature writing is mostly a crafting research-based story with color, characters, development, well structural arc good writers or journalists engage as their uniforms. When feature writers succeed at this, the writing is placed in a context of obtaining the element of the feature or news article.

CHAPTER THREE

FEATURE AND ITS AUXILIARIES

Characteristics in Journalistic or Feature Writing

Whether you are writing a feature article or a news story, you must always consider the below listed characteristics though they may not be limited to the media landscape, especially with the emergence of sophistication and the social media. Feature writing is a profession that is acquired over a period of time. In that direction, proper training modules are required to prepare a renounced writer into a feature writer. To achieve this task will only be possible through a vigorous professional and comprehensive course of study in journalism or mass communication.

Just as in news gathering and writing, the characteristics have not changed. They remain the same as listed below:

- Accuracy
- Balance
- Clarity
- Precision
- Efficiency

Exercise: It is an undisputable fact that you may have come across the above listed characteristics while doing communication course in news gathering and writing. Notwithstanding, explain the above listed words (characteristics) according to your learning or understanding and give examples. (*A brain Teaser*)

Types of Features

As you have been informed in earlier discussion, a feature story is distinguished from other types of non-fiction by the quality of the writing. After going through the basic concept on the elements of feature, let us now do a more pragmatic approach through a diversified means depending on the situation or issue as it relates to feature writing. On this note, the below are the various types of features based on their applications and situations;

Personality profile: - Often a human-interest feature takes on greater depth and turns into a personality feature. In many instances, the personality feature resembles a characterization. The main character may be known or unknown but will have done something of interest to others. Maybe, the person developed a product that has become an international retail item; learned to overcome shyness and became a political candidate; goes to school each day on kekeh, Penpen, Aboboyaa or Okada (motto cycle or tri cycle). Usually the personality features show how a person gained recognition.

According to Hutchison (2007) personality profile is a feature that propels the feature writer to pin or write on the personality of people. That is, the writer is mostly concern about featuring the person; there is no form of optimism or stratification. All you do is to write about the individual in question. Please note that a personality profile is different from that of a personality sketch or curriculum vitae, in that the personality profile is handled in a broader manner where you make the writing colorful to reflect a feature writing/article.

Example:(*Just an introduction*) *Ms. Shirley Andrews, a onetime brilliant student of the Samuel Memorial Doe Institute (SMDI) in Duala, Liberia has become an educational icon in Liberia by winning this year's international essay competition netting her Two Thousand United States*

Dollars (US$2000.00) something she never dreamt of.(**Can you attempt completing this article?**)

Human Interest: -The most common of the feature articles, the human-interest feature does exactly what it says: describes some unusual aspect of the life of an ordinary human being, an aspect which makes him or her interesting. Sometimes the story reports success in spite of great odds. Sometimes it recalls a tragic predicament. Sometimes it shares a continuing struggle supported only by hope and faith. For instance, a story of African Peace keepers deployed to keep peace and stability in Syria in the midst of heavy bombardment and some of the peace keepers met with their demise in combat helps readers see the complexity of human emotion during war.

Human interest feature makes or evokes the readers emotionally, depresses, stimulates, entertains or arouses them. As in straight news, most features have human interest elements. Imagine a situation in two different communities that are faced with health hazard from a pile of dirt say for instance, Sonii Wein in Liberia and Kru Town Road in Sierra Leone. To write a good feature piece on these precarious situations, you have to first contact stakeholders or residents of those communities and health authorities concerned. By this, you will be able to collect your data and analytically write an evoking feature that will captivate the emotion of the readers.

An example introduction paragraph for the Sonii When scenario in Liberia: *A community almost close to the central part of the capital city Monrovia, in terms Of proximity, Sonii Wein a host of the much talked about market in the city popularly known as Rally Town Market is almost at the verge of being deserted due to pungent (stinky odor) as a result of the heavy pile of garbage on the main street in the Sonii Wein Community may impede the free flow of vehicles to other communities.*

An example introduction paragraph for the Kru Town Road situation in Freetown: *As people walk down the street of Kru Town Road in Freetown, they are greeted by odor of offence smell due to the stock pile of garbage that has taken over a onetime street (Kru Town Road)* *habitable environment and considered a recreational hub for the youths of Freetown, Sierra Leone.*

Historical subjects feature: -Sometimes historical features focus on historical events or celebrations. Stemming usually from library research, such features provide human-interest history lessons. Historical feature deals with issues reflective of current realities but gives some historical dimension. For instance, if a feature writer wants to bring to memory the infamous April 14 "rice riot" in Liberia or the 1986 "students riot" in Kaduna, Nigeria, the writer will resonate the past events by the trying to write on current events or issues that have similar current occurrences and write in context to reflect previous happenings to make it current, especially where issues dealing with are similar to those that occurred in Liberia and Nigeria over two decades ago. This is where the lead or introduction will strive to arouse or have impact on the reader, either to be interested in the article or not. The essence of historical feature is to create fresh memories in the minds of the readers.

Example On the Liberian scenario (Introduction paragraph):*With the persistence scarcity of commodities on the Liberian market, especially rice the country's staple food might result to the recurrence of the April 14 rice riot in 1979 when thousands of Liberians took to the streets of Monrovia to demonstrate against the pronounced increment in the price of fifty kilo bag of rice a situation that brought the country to a standstill for almost two months.*

Example for the Kaduna episode (An introduction paragraph):As media reports continue to highlight the current wave of students protest over the speculated increase in tuition across the Northern region of Nigeria in Kaduna, if urgent remedy is not taken by the government, the situation might generate to a repeat of the 1986 students riot in Kaduna which left scores of persons dead.

Seasonal Feature: - Seasonal features deal mainly with important occasions or holidays such as Christmas, New Year, Independence,

Ramadan or other memorable holidays. The writer of such a feature reflects on events of the past but places same in current perspective.

Example: *As the Christmas fever grips people all over the world particularly Christian nations, Liberians in their numbers are in high gear of preparation to celebrate joyfully, especially coming from a peaceful and successful 2017 presidential and legislative elections.*

Elements of Feature

In addition to the various elements you have learned, either directly or indirectly in news gathering and writing, the below listed elements may provide you with a broader in-depth and understanding of the general elements in writing a feature article considering elements of feature, just as in **physical science,** where any of the four substances *air, fire, water* and *earth* are formerly believed to compose of or constitute the physical universe, so you have in feature writing for now the below listed five elements. They are;

- ❖ Human Interest
- ❖ Curiosity
- ❖ Suspense
- ❖ Relevance
- ❖ Conflict

Human Interest: is an article that is of human concern, where the article evokes the emotion and feelings of those affected or readers to effectuate a change.

Curiosity: This is where you write to create, arouse interest or generate interest in others affairs. In a local parlance, you want to know about others and write about them.

Suspense: This is a state where your writing makes the readers to be of mental uncertainty. You live your readers in a state of not actually getting the real ending of your writing but yet projects meaning to them.

Relevance: Your feature writing must be of relativity to the subject matter. What is of significant or important to the issue you trying to covey.

Conflict: Your writing must be in an antagonistic form or a divergent of ideals or issues but with no attack on persons' personality.

In feature writing you use these elements to lure the interest of the readers. As you may have understood earlier, these elements play or represent the same functions as in basic news writing. To just emphasize a bit on accuracy, credible and balance reporting aimed at creating a harmonious society, following years of practice in the field of journalism and tutorage in several universities, particularly at the state owned university (University of Liberia), a theory was developed to serve as a guide for practicing and would be journalists.

It is an opportunity to have same (theory) reflected in this book. The theory is the "**SPE Anderson theory of communication**" meaning that, no matter where you find yourself as a mass communicator or journalist, you must always have the instinct that there exist **society, people** and **events**(SPE) where there is a symbiotic relationship amongst them. That is, a society must exist where people are living and interacting through events (activities).

In this regard, as a journalist or mass communicator living in any given society as part of the three, you are the conduit that society depends on for the conveyance of information and transformation. Therefore, as you carry out your journalistic function either through news reporting or feature writing, you are opportune as an interpreter since you are a part of the "Society, People, and Event" (SPE) to be placed in a vantage position to observe the relationship among the three, and as a conduit, report in the interest of the popular majority in an effort aimed at promoting mutual coexistence and *harmony*. (*The bullet and stone will not recognize you as a journalist or mass communicator in the event of chaos or protestation therefore, you must always strive to promote and maintain the harmonization of society through your reportage*).

Case Study 1

A war Is being fought between two warring factions in a country at two extreme fronts where hundreds of their own armed men (fighters) and civilians are killed and thousands worth of properties damaged. This pathetic situation claimed the attention of the international community. A regional peace keeping force was organized and deployed by the Authority of the region to quell the situation and also to maintain peace; but with all the efforts made, the two factions remain adamant and recalcitrant in their quest to defeat each other for supremacy.

At the same time, atrocities and mayhem continued to be permeated in every facet of the country where even the peace keepers were gravely affected. It happens that an interim government was put in place by the same Authority of the region to herald for peace. With all of these developments, one of the factions from a distance location was not in favor of the interim government and decided to wage an all-out war to destabilize the interim government by attacking same with a rain of rackets. While in the process, innocent people and some of the same peace keepers were killed not hitting the target where the interim government was operating or situated was missed.

*You are a journalist stringing or filing report for any of the international broadcasting institutions may be, the Voice of America (VOA), Radio France International (RFI) or British Broadcasting Corporation (BBC) living and operating within the domain of the interim government. While filing your report to your media institution the next day regarding the attack on the interim government by the disgruntled faction, you reported through broadcast that the perceived enemy faction from the distance missed target by <u>ten feet</u> to have hit the location of the interim government. (How do you see this report, is it a good one, or is it in line with the "SPE Anderson theory of communication")? Check it out. Looking back at your report, what would you have done differently?*Based on this case study, you must always be knowledgeable of your reportage and the society including the people you are reporting on or for. Equally so, your report/writing should create curiosity for the readers as you try to report on strange events or odd situations. Many a time, readers look forward to strange and unusual things not only in your environment but also in different parts of the world. Your reporting must be relevant to the situation, especially people and events you reporting on. And of course, without the existence of the "SPE", there will be no conflict and without conflict there will be no harmony. But as a reporter, journalist or mass communicator *always opt for the harmony of society.*

Characteristics of Feature Stories

No matter what issue or idea you are writing on, the following are some of the most important characteristics of feature stories. They may inform, instruct and advise, but their primary purpose is to entertain and inform the readers. Features are usually read after the news and in leisure moments.

- They are factual, and require reporting.
- They may or may not be timely. If they are timely and related to a current news event, they are likely to appeal more to readers.
- They may be written in any form and style. The only criterion is that the form and style be appropriate to the contents and purpose of the story.
- They permit the reporter to use his/her knowledge and ingenuity to write a story original in ideas and treatment.
- They rarely have news leads. Instead, they more often have novelty leads.
- They usually strike the keynote in the opening sentences, which permit the readers to come into quick contact with the story and become interested.
- They usually are not cut in make-up. Thus, the reporter may use any device of the fiction writer: suspense, dialogue, description, narration, climax, and the like. The inverted pyramid does not fit the purpose of a feature story.
- They require the writer to apply his/her imaginations to the facts, yet they are not fiction.
- Tilley applies to all principles of effective writing to achieve unity, coherence, and emphasis.
- They bring readers as close as possible to the experience or idea of the story which the reader feels himself as a part of the story.

Qualities of a Feature Story

In evaluating the qualities of a feature story Lewis (2003) enumerated the below qualities:

- ✓ Feature stories are descriptive and full of detail information of interest.
- ✓ Feature stories generally have a strong narrative posture.
- ✓ Feature stories have a strong lead that grabs the attention of readers.
- ✓ Feature stories often depend on interviews for your attributions.
- ✓ Feature stories include quotations from the person(s) involved.
- ✓ Feature stories combine facts and opinion, with a focus on the human interest side of the story.
- ✓ Feature stories educate, entertain and at times inform. They can include colorful detail as well as humor.
- ✓ Feature stores contain the voice of the writer.
- ✓ Feature stories can be organized in a variety of ways (i.e., chronologically, narrative fashion).

The Usage of Simple Words

This aspect of the book is not intended to bore you reading a lesson in English, but rather intended to refresh your memories as you strive to become a mass communicator or an astute journalist. In this regard, in order to achieve your goal as an effective communicator or writer, it is always good to use simple words. Most people don't believe that simple words are the most powerful and effective means that can be used in any journalistic writing for smooth and effective communication. If you want to get your message across to readers/listeners, express yourself in the simplest way possible. Many people believe the opposite. They think by using more complex and elaborate words, the more effective the message becomes.

In furtherance to improving your writing skills as a feature writer or journalist, you must possess the ability to use the language efficiently, effectively and with confidence which are the hallmark of a good journalist or writer. You are also under obligation to learn certain writing techniques and structures to be successful, but those requirements do not reduce or lessen the creativity of the writing process.

Techniques of Writing the Feature

Just as in the normal essay writing, feature writing is of no exception in its package. The below are the format used in writing a feature piece.

Structure: - A feature is seldom written in the traditional inverted pyramid pattern. Feature may be written in a narrative fashion, much like a good joke of anecdote. The good feature requires as much organization as the straight news story, for the feature has to flow smoothly and parts of a feature story must be kept intact if it is to succeed. In the well-planned story, every paragraph, every sentence, should add to the total effect.

Leads: -The lead most attract immediate attention and pull the reader into the story. Leads can vary in style and content. You can use description, narration, dialogue, question, unusual statement, call to action, comparison-contrast. *Transition:* -No matter how good the lead is, you need a solid transition into the body of the feature. If you think of the lead as a lure to attract the audience, then the transition will set the hook. It makes the reader want to continue. And it promises some kind of satisfaction or reward. The reward can be entertainment, information or self- awareness but has to be something of value to the reader.

Body: -Sound knowledge of the subject, coupled with good writing skills, will let you take the reader through a variety of experiences. You should use the standard writing devices of crisp dialogue, documentable but vivid fact and detail, careful observation, suspense and if appropriate, plot.

Conclusions: -The conclusion should give the reader a sense of satisfaction you need to tie the conclusion to the lead so that the story has unity. Often you can do this through a short, tight summary, occasionally, you can conclude with an anecdote or a quote that sums up the substance of the story. With a narrative approach, you build toward a climax.

Length: - If a reporter asks how long a feature story should be. The editor may reply, "as long as you keep it interesting." Feature stories vary in length from two or three paragraphs to 10 or 15 triple-spaced sheets of copy. Reader's interest is the main yardstick by which they are judged. And editors are paid to accurately assess, readers interest.

The Difference Between Feature and News Story

The writing styles of a news story and a feature are different. In a news story, the emphasis is on content rather than form. **News stories** go straight to the point, using simple and effective words to deliver the facts quickly. They usually are concerned with the normal 5 "W" and 1 "H". New stories have a strait jacket posture.

Things to Consider When Writing A Feature Piece

As stated earlier, feature writing is an analytical writing that demands the best out of the writer and to achieve this goal, you must write in perspective.

Below are few points to give you guidance:

Point 1. Story mapping
The first thing you do as a feature writer is exploration of all possible angles for instance, if you are writing a feature on university students center discos as they are popularly known in some parts of Africa, then you need to make a list of issues concerning campus based discos. This may include the kind of students center that run the disco, the ambience at the disco, the bands that play at the disco, the background of teenagers who flock to the disco, the dress they wear, their mannerisms, the prevalence of drugs or drinks culture at the disco.

Point 2. Decide your angle
You can't possibly write a feature on African universities that cover all the point listed above. Such a feature will either become too long or

too generalized. It makes sense to narrow your feature down to two or three points on the same issue.

Point 3. Break down each point into several sub- points

If you have decided to focus on teenagers who crowd such disco, then you can build sub themes such as:

Dressing: How do these teenagers dress? Is it in keeping with the general social trends or it is different? Being out specific styles favored by groups?

Age group: What is their age group?

Average spends: How much money do they spend on a single day or night?
What are the products that they buy? Is it drinks, food or drugs?

Background: Are the people that go to the students' center discos students?
Are they working professional? Are they married?

Hair style: How about their hair style? Are they premed? Are they spiked?

Point 4. Start your research

Obviously, the first place to visit in such an occurrence is the students' center disco. Meet with the stakeholders including the disco manager, waiters, Disco jokey, (DJ) with the aim of speaking to them at length to get details about how the dressing, attitudes and mannerism of disco goers. Next, speak to a cross section of dancers, make sure you get to speak to collegians, working couples, single men and women. Find out about their backgrounds, and the reasons that bring them to the disco. Speak to their parents, friend if possible. Speak to the police. Find out if there are brawls, scuffles, drug taking at the discos, and if yes, what is the background of youths involved.

Point 5. Search the information and put on your thinking cap:

Always remember that feature is not a news story, which has to be written in an inverted pyramid format. You have to relate your feature as a story teller. Your goal should be to convey or transport your readers to a student's center disco and let them visualize groups of teenagers, working people, single girls gyrating to music under glittering lights. They should be able to recreate scene simply by reading your feature.

This can happen only if your description is accurate and realistic. It is not enough to say that young boys and girls from different families are making a beeline to student's centers discos. It is important to describe a 15 – something girl in a short top climbing on the arms of her boyfriend with spiked hair as they make their way to the dance floor. It is essential to describe the brand of cigarette a young man is smoking as he stares at single girls and make smoke rings. Notwithstanding, make sure you stick to the themes that you have selected. Your feature should not stray into areas that are not relevant to your immediate focus. Also please put your opinions on the backburner. Your job is not to moralize, but to narrate a story; you should use quotes to add color and drama to your feature article.

Point 6. Punch line:

I am sure you have heard about most of the world boxers like Mick Tyson, Mohamed Allie, or Cassius Clay among others. In feature writing, you are a boxer of information always wanting to release information punches for consumption. Make sure your round off the feature with suitable punch line. This can be a quote or a wise crack, knowing that it should be in keeping with the theme of your feature article.

Prewriting the Feature Article

Before you can write a good feature piece, it is important to follow the below listed steps though they may not be limited to your writing:

Step 1. Finding the story

If you are not assigned a subject by your editor, your search begins with finding the right topic. Your topic should be related to breaking news or current issues or trends. Seeing a good topic for a feature article in the midst of hard news depends on your curiosity and hard work. In short, your creativity determines how you will deal with an issue or subject.

For instance, if the breaking news deals with students demonstration on the campus, your feature story may result from an interview with stakeholders of the university who will give you authentic information on the occurrence. Or your feature story may result from a personal tour of the campus, noting impact resulted from the demonstration, reporting students and professors affected, and observing classrooms damaged. Remember, feature articles usually evoke some kind of emotion. Finding the human interest aspect of hard news leads you to feature articles.

Step 2. Gathering the Information

Whether the information comes from your own account, interviews with eyewitnesses, or printed sources, you must gather as much information as possible. Even though a feature article is not a straight news story, its facts must be accurate and its message valid for reliability.

Step 3. Determining the type of Feature

Your purpose determines the type of feature you will write. Features are limited only by the writer/reporter's conceptualization; however, you came across a few basic types of features suggested in your earlier reading.

Step 4. Choosing the Single Focus

When you have determined your purpose (and, thus, the kind of feature you plan to write), force yourself to write a single sentence that explains the specific focus the article will take. Although this sentence probably will not appear in the article, it will help you frame your thoughts. The sentence may look as something like this: *Some African university students majoring in mass communication are preparing to assume greater responsibility on the international space to become media managers or experts.*

Step 5. Determining the Organization of the Feature

Decide how you can best present the information in your feature. Will an order of importance be best? Will a flashback work better? Will chronological order be better? Will coherent be of importance? Keep in mind that you are communicating through feature article for your reader to understand you.

Step 6. Drafting the Lead

The lead, or introduction, must catch the reader's attention and make him or her want to read more. Use any attention-getting device suitable to your topic. Make sure, too, that the lead sets the tone for the article. Examples of leads:

- Asking a question or questions
- Making an unusual statement
- Describing a scene
- Presenting a conversation
- Telling a brief story
- Presenting surprising or alarming statistics
- Referring to an event, either historical or current
- Showing a controversy or contradiction
- Using a quotation, adage, or proverb
- Stating an unusual opinion
- Dialogue

Step 7. Drafting the Body

Following the organizational pattern you selected in Step 5 above, develop the body of the feature article. Keep in mind the creative nature of the feature, and realize that your best tool for writing is an inquisitive mind. Use techniques appropriate to short-story writing and strive to achieve an easy style.

Step 8. Drafting the Conclusion

The conclusion of a feature article is much like the conclusion of any short story. It gives an air of finality and ties together any loose ends. It may also refer back to the lead. It usually does not, however, end with a summary or conclusion in the manner of a traditional expository composition.

Step 9. Preparing the Headline

Sometimes most feature writers through intuition, have the opportunity to develop their own headlines; in other cases editors or someone else assumes this responsibility. When you develop your own as a feature writer, you should add a headline which attracts reader attention and pinpoints the focus of your article.

Step 10. Checking for Good Writing Techniques

Since the feature article is more nearly creative writing than anything else, revise the piece according to the below suggestions:

- Does the article reflect careful complete research?
- Do I attract my reader's attention in the opening paragraph? (see the types of leads)
- Does the article maintain interest throughout?
- Did I follow a logical organization to achieve my purpose?
- Have I maintained unity?
- Have I varied sentence structure in keeping with the tone and purpose?
- Are transitions sufficient to guarantee smooth reading?
- Does the word choice show freshness and originality?
- Have I eliminated wordiness? Always think about word economy

CHAPTER FOUR

WRITING THE FEATURE

Before writing any feature story or article, you must first have the concept and from which you will produce a headline. The headline is the most vital part of your feature. Treat the headline as if it were a summary of the article. Ask yourself, Why is this story important? What about it, will it grab readers' interest? A good headline answers those questions by telling the reader something new, different or useful.

To come up with a good headline, pretend you're telling a friend what the article is all about, explaining the most interesting aspects of your story. Keep the wording simple, and avoid superlatives and emotive language. Also, avoid using a brand or client's name in the headline unless it is very well known. Instead, focus on what is most interesting about your topic.

Even though there is a greater freedom in writing a feature article as compared to that of the straight or traditional news story, the feature writer should keep in mind the basic elements of structure so that the feature article or story will have unity and coherence. Remember that just as in exploratory or essay writing, where you have three major parts, including the introduction, body and conclusion, the lead in feature writing is considered as the introduction. In contrast to the inverted pyramid style of writing a straight news story, the structure of a feature article requires proper planning, and it resembles that of a spool.

As in other writings, writing a feature story article requires proper planning, much consideration and critical revision, which is not a bad thing to do. There is not much a difference from feature interview to those of other purposes, especially the straight news stories. With news stories, the interviewers look for hints and utterances or words. They look for how words are said and not what is said.

Feature articles or stories are more immanent or subjective and full of emotion. Feature articles mostly focus on contemporary issues or topic with specificity publish in newspaper or magazine. They generally present information in a more narratorial way to make them more engaging with the readers. As you venture to understanding all about feature writing, it is important to know that the process involved in writing the article will differ from one situation to the other, but generally the writing follows a logical production sequence. On this premise, your feature story begins with an issue or idea, if not several of them mixed in together.

Sometimes feature articles emanate from the regular straight news, something you overheard issues, or something you observed happenings in your community or locale. Those initial ideas or issues could be of insignificant or small and vague or big and clear. If you think there is consumable or saleable story in them, you will be at will to find out some detailed information and develop a topic proposal, or story, to send to an editor of the news organ. Or, most often, the editor comes out with the idea for you to develop.

The next stage is work out a feasible or practical work plan. From practical experience, before writing a feature story, you ask yourself questions like, who am I to speak to, and where to go to source the information from? In feature writing, you will not write a good feature piece without interviewing several people who I refer to as stakeholders. These are knowledgeable of the issue or idea you are dealing with in your feature story, and as a must, you also must get out to where the action is for you to get first-hand information regarding your feature article.

In feature writing, it is always good to have a recorder with you to record your interviews because at some point, while preparing for the actual writing of your feature article, you will have to transcribe recorded interviews, assimilate or digesting notes gathered from the field as it will play on the page. Note that in writing a feature story, you do not deal with several issues or ideas in your article. You must deal with one issue, no disjointed issues, for instance, if you are dealing with the causes responsible for Africa's under development, though there will be several causes but your central focus and idea will be concentrated on "under development".

The Structure of a Feature

As stated earlier, like any other form of writing, a feature story or article in professional local parlance follows the same standard format or structure. However, the format or structure may vary depending on the issue you are dealing with or your topic, no matter the issue or topic, a feature article should always consist of a headline, introduction, the main body, and a concluding paragraph. In a more professional context, it can safely be stated that a feature structure or format is a general-purpose information structure that identifies and groups together individual features, each of which associates an identity or name with one or more values. In this context, the structure of a feature article includes the below listed:

- ➢ Headline
- ➢ Secondary headline
- ➢ The controlling idea
- ➢ Lead
- ➢ Body
- ➢ Close
- ➢ Imagery or quotation
- ➢ Any additional components

To have a clearer understanding, have a brief knowledge on each of the above format or structures of an appreciable feature article or story:

Headline - The headline is the catchy title of your feature story or article. It provides a quick hint at the topic and is found at the top location of the feature article. Its purpose is to arouse the interest of readers and to grab their attention. In other to accomplish this mission, your headline must be catchy and intriguing.

Secondary Headline - The secondary headline gives more information about the topic and should include the angle and controlling idea of your feature article. While the headline is meant to attract readers, the secondary headline is a little bit more **serious**. Its purpose is to give the reader(s) a more precise idea of what they will read about.

The Controlling Idea - The controlling idea originates from angling or angle. Just as in straight or tradition news writing, controlling idea tells the reader(s) what they will read about, and the feature article is going in. It can be a difficult thing to grasp the idea at first, but the controlling idea is quite a simple one. Think of it as where your feature article will take the reader. It is a further narrowing down of the angle the feature is taking. It may act as a kind of guideline for the audience, something for them to keep in mind as they are reading your article.

The Lead – is an opening paragraph which summarizes the story. The lead gives readers the most important information of the news story in a clear concise and interesting form or manner. In short, the lead is the opening paragraph of your feature article, and it should include the angle of the feature article and the controlling idea. It should be written in a way to hook the readers, in a way that it generates interest that will encourage them read the rest of the article. The lead can be written in any form or manner, but the way it turns out depends on you the writer.

To write a good and captivating lead, there are two things you should put into consideration. They are:

- The lead must entice or hook your reader(s) attention. To achieve this goal, you must consider the following:

Humor – is a best way to attract your reader(s). This can be done through jokes and puns, this geared towards setting a light tone for what is to come.

Anecdotes – They give the reader(s) something to quickly grasp by helping them set up the idea or issue. By using examples, anecdotes enable readers to visualize the issue.

The use of Description – describing a situation, feeling or event in your feature story, tells or conveys a whole lot of emotion on the reader(s).

Facts or Statistics – When these are presented with punch, can instantly interest a reader into wanting to know more what is your feature story is all about.

- The lead must include the angle and the controlling idea:

The angle of feature must be noticed; Though the wording does not need to be the same, the angle does need to be mentioned in the lead.

The controlling idea must be present; If this is present in your feature lead, the readers will not know what they are reading about. They need to be given something to care about or look forward to learning about, otherwise, they will lose interest and disengage thereby living them in oblivion.

The Body of the Feature - At this stage of your educational surgeon, you are quite cognizant about the body of an essay. Just in case it has slipped off from the cerebrum, the body is where you present the issue of your feature article to the reader(s). It is the bulk of the article where you present your case. At this stage of your educational surgeon, you are quite cognizant about the body of an essay. Just in case it has slipped off from the cerebrum, the body is where you present the issue of your feature article to the reader(s). It is the bulk of the article where you present your case.

You the writer are the one to determine the way the article is to be structured. The information found in the feature article can be organized in many ways. Below are few examples to direct your path to writing a good feature piece:

Cause and effect: Please note that your feature article is all about presenting information by describing the cause of an issue you are propounding through the provision of context that is, major players or stakeholders and events featuring in your feature article and then showing its effect or impact on the involved people, environment, businesses, or organization.

Problem-solution: Your information is presented by describing a problem within a framework or context of your feature and ending with a possible solution that would possibly impact your reader(s).

From the general to specific: The information of your article is presented from a wide context to more specific points of the issue.

Chronologically: Your information is presented through time and in a chronological manner.

Logically: Your feature article must demonstrate logical issue, clear, and coherent for the reader. Minus this, your reader(s) will not follow your idea.

The Close – May be this could be the first time coming across this word (close) in your professional pursuit. The close is last paragraph of the feature article. When utilized in your article, it must leave a lasting impact or impression on your reader(s). Please understand that the close is not the last paragraph of your feature article, and therefore, it is not the conclusion. Do not use it by starting "Finally" or "In concluding". One way to leave a lasting impression or impact on your reader(s) is to circle back to your lead or the headline. For example, if you used an anecdote in the lead, you may want to mention the anecdote again in the close, now taking the information you have presented into consideration.

The use of Quotation or **imagery** – This plays an important role in feature writing. A quotation is derived from source texts, and it is often stake holders who are knowledgeable in the issue you are dealing with in your feature article. Quotation creates imagery and gives weight and importance to your feature article. In other to give seriousness to your article, it is paramount that you include at least one or two quotations in you feature article. Understand that there are two types of quotation in feature writing. They are:

- *Direct quotation* – This is a quotation that comes from a person's or stakeholder's exact words that are used in your article. You must mention the person quoted "as is". In news writing, it is referred to as "attribution", which at is used as *according to*.

  Whereas, in feature article, you directly quote the person such as Richmond Sayou, a university lecturer, stressed the need for "university students to be studious and committed to academic surgeon if they are to positively contribute to the agenda of national development".

- *Indirect quotation* – This is where you as a feature writer will paraphrase the stakeholder's words. An indirect quote must also acknowledge the stakeholder from whom the idea has been taken. You can mention the stakeholder before or after the quotation such as, Richmond Sayou a university lecturer, has stressed the need for university students to be studious and committed in their educational surgeon if they are to contribute positively to the agenda of national development.

How to Write a Feature Article?

To write a good feature piece, it is necessary to consider the below listed point:

1. Write a hook to open your story
2. Expand on your lead in the second paragraph
3. Follow your outline
4. Show, don't tell
5. Don't use too many quotes
6. Choose language that is appropriate to your re
7. Keep your opinion out of the article
8. Revise your article.

Key Tips for Writing a Good Feature

Before starting your feature article, you must consider the following Tips:

- o Conceptualize the issue/idea you want to write on;
- o From which institution or environment are you focusing the writing on for your article;
- o What are the real issues you want to deal with;
- o Identify the actors or stakeholders involved with the daily functioning of the institution you are focusing or featuring;
- o Jot down the points you want to get information on from each concerned stakeholder;

Do your research by gathering your information or data.

With the above condition met, you now have an idea on how to write a feature article. It is undisputable that most of you reading this book, especially students pursuing their academic surgeon in mass communication or journalism, will agree that you came across the basic elements to write a composition or essay. However, feature writing is a different terrain. In this vein, writing a good feature requires an intellectual warm up by referring to your academic morgue, especially English, with emphasis on grammar.

Little Things to Remember as a Feature Writer

In order to write an appealing feature, remember few of the things you learned years back while you were in high or secondary school. They include:

- ➢ Grammar
- ➢ Phrases
- ➢ Research
- ➢ Illustration
- ➢ Description
- ➢ Specific
- ➢ Tone
- ➢ Revision

Just in case you might have forgotten though, let's zoom through the above listed.

Grammar: In its simplistic form, grammar is the set of rules that explain how words are used in a language. By dictionary reference, grammar is the study of the classes of words, their inflections, and their functions and relations in the sentence.

Example: Female students in communication 315 class (photo journalism) are learning the grammar of filmmaking.

Phrases: A short written or spoken expression. Grammatically, a phrase is a word or group of words that functions as a single unit in the syntax of a sentence, usually consisting of a head, or central word and elaborating words.

Research: Is a frantic or diligent inquiry or examination to seek facts on that which is unknown or known (known in this application is to revise existing facts), a laborious or continued search after the truth.

Illustration: This is the act of showing (illustrating) or making something or an issue clear and distinct.

Description: This is a vivid sketch or account of anything in words, portraiture or an enumeration of the essential qualities of something.

Specific: This is where you have to be explicit or definite on the issue you dealing with, that is pinning on a particular issue from the general.

Tone: There are many meanings for this word, ranging from music to literature. For our purpose in context of literature, tone is the manner in which speech or your writing is expressed.

Revision: This is the action or process of editing, reviewing or amending a written piece. (Read and read over until you are satisfied for release to the readers). This is very important in feature written.

The Purpose of Feature Writing

If you give yourself a moment to ponder on the role of the media, you will come to the realization that the news media is an informational tool to achieve the communication goal of organization or people. One useful writing material used to achieve this is feature article. Features are more in-depth than traditional news stories and go beyond providing the most important facts. The purpose of these stories is to provide a detailed description of a place, person, idea, or organization. Although reporters and editors classify features as news stories, they are not necessarily structured using the inverted pyramid style. Instead, features use storytelling devices to help the reader connect with the overall narrative and its central characters. Features are particularly common in newspaper and magazine writing, although they frequently appear in other media.

Profiles or personality features that give insight into a person's role, experience, or background are one type of feature. Among the most common subjects of profiles are celebrities, athletes, individuals who overcome challenges, and high-profile executives. It is important to understand the circumstances that warrant a feature piece from a strategic communication perspective. Communication professionals write feature articles to provide in-depth exposure for their client or organization.

A feature can increase a client or company's visibility and even help find new key audiences. If you need to quickly get information about your client or organization to the media, a feature article or story may not be the best tool because it is typically longer than a traditional news story. However, you could write a feature article on, for example, your university's new chancellor or president to provide more background information to key audiences. Feature stories are also used in an organization's internal communications, such as newsletters and magazines.

Overall, feature articles use an informative tone while incorporating creative and descriptive devices in order to increase audience taste or appeal. Furthermore, feature article is to explore or discuss a particular topic of interest. It is subjective and demonstrates either the opinion of the composer or the various opinions of community groups aimed at providing information of interest.

What is a Feature in Journalism?

Feature in journalism is a write-up in a newspaper or magazine article or report of a person, event, an aspect of a major event, or the like, often having a personal slant and written in an individual style. Compare follow-up the main or most prominent story in a magazine. Feature in journalism gives the writer a state of unlimited scope to express his or her analytical thoughts on events that will stimulate the curiosity of the readers.

What is a Feature Agile?

An agile is an active or quick development in a feature that contains a chunk of functionality that delivers business value. Features can include additions or changes to existing functionality. For planning purposes, some agile methodologies also use the notion of "work items" that can include features, bug fixes, documents, and other artifacts. A feature article in newspaper is the main story in the magazine or newspaper that a feature focuses on a special event, place or person in great detail. There are many types of feature articles, whether they are creatively focused or newsworthy, however, they always have one thing in common which is human interest.

Who is a Feature Writer?

What does a feature writer do? No matter your stance or the condition, your job as a feature writer is using the written word to tell true stories that inform, entertain and persuade people. A feature story typically is a long, in-depth article that is written using a mix of news writing and narrative storytelling techniques.

Expected Words in a Feature Article?

The number of words in a feature article is usually dependent on theingenuity of the feature writer. While most feature articles are at least 500 words in length, the editor may decide that they need something a bit shorter due to page layout. Also, don't be surprised if some of your features end up being 2000 words or more. The best thing you can do in this case is to take advice from the editor you are working with or depending on the issue you are dealing with may even warrant writing up to 3000 words.

What is a User Story?

A user story is a chunk of functionality (some people use the word feature) that is of value to the customer or reader. What you call a feature is usually referred to as theme or epic. Themes and epics are used to group user stories to bigger feature sets that make sense on their own.

User story according to McKane(2006)is a description of objective, which helps a person to achieve a feature. So that he/she is able to utilize that feature when using software application. User story is a part of agile development process. Every process has some characteristics which makes it clear and concise.

Additional Tips for Feature Writing

Below are some basic tips for people who are beginning to write feature:

Cover the essential elements of who, what, when, where, how and why;
Put the most important things at the beginning, preferably in the first paragraph;
Plan out what you are going to say beforehand;
Look at your chosen theme carefully. Consider the questions suggested and attempt to answer some of them;

Remember, just as in straight news writing, you need an "angle" that is, the direction to focus your feature. You cannot answer all of those questions.

This is journalism, and journalism needs to be new and original. That is why an "angle" is important: even if your topic has been covered in the past, there will always be something new to say and you need quotes or attributions to give your feature piece a better characterization and imageries.

Planning the Feature Lead

A strong lead paragraph offers intrigue from the start. Editors don't have time to read through the entire article to reach your key point, and neither do your readers. Think of the lead as an extended version of the headline, even using some of the same words. When writing a lead, try to keep the paragraph short at most two to three short sentences. In total, your feature should be close to 400 or more words. Do not bother about your brand at this point; just introduce the interesting aspects of the story. If your lead reads like an advertisement or announcement, it will be discarded immediately.

You should know that there is no undertaken the world over without planning. As you were informed earlier in this book, the focal point of a feature article is to create impact on the readers. As such, your feature lead or introduction must be well written to catch the attention of the readers. This can only be achieved through proper planning and concentration. Readers' mind can only be alert on issues when they are fed with piecing and interesting information through your writing. In the absence of this, the mind of the readers will be oblique and coupled with traumatic effect. As a feature writer, you have something to tell readers. Therefore, your first sentence or paragraph must be attention catching to penetrate their minds. This will captivate them and take them from their wonderland.

Note that the feature lead must attract attention. It must be nothing but the truth as it relates to the issue (article) you are writing on.

Types of Feature Leads

In order to be meticulous and project intriguing feature piece, it is important to be familiar with some leads that would provide writing guidance for your article(s). McKinney (1986) notes there are four types of feature which I will endeavor to explain as far my understanding is concerned.

For this writing, below are the four leads that may be useful in feature writing:-

Striking statement lead
Summary lead
Question lead
Narrative Anecdote lead

Understanding the various leads

Striking Statement Lead: - In its noun form, strike is a work or function stoppage by a body of workers that warrants enforcement and compliance with demands made on an employer (Murray, 2003).

With this insight, as a feature writer you must demand from your readers their interest to read your article. This is where it becomes necessary to use the striking **lead.** The striking lead is a lead whose opening sentence or statement must be of attention grabbing geared toward arousing anxiety or curiosity. It is advisable to most of the time use the unusual fact of events.

Example: James Anderson, a high school graduate, born in one of the remotest villages in Liberia has become one of the world's richest, a situation he never imagined.

The Summary Lead: - This lead includes a number of ideas or aspects that may start with an overall summary statement that may claim the attention of the reader.

Example: Despite the many challenges experienced by most African students as a result of the global economic constraints, yet still they are performing remarkably well in their academic pursuit a situation that is hailed by some educators in the continent.

Please note that in feature writing, you are at will to propound different ideas in the introduction statement (lead) something that is unusual in straight news writing.

The Question Lead: - As the word question applies, this lead always ask question on the issue you are writing on. In this stead, the question lead must be written with caution because it sometimes creates problem that cannot be easily solved in the article. However, if skillfully applied, the question lead can cause to evoke or arouse the attention of the reader. A question lead could be appropriate when use in line with explanatory statement that makes an assertion or explain a situation about which question to be asked.

Example: Most probably it will never happen to you, but just in case you are seriously injured on your campus while rushing to class and got collided with some of your colleagues at the entrance of your class; This could mean months at the hospital and may be an unfortunate situation to drop from the university, in the event of this mishap, where would you get money from to defray your hospital bill, and meet up with your cost of living?

The Narrative or Anecdote Lead: - The narrative or anecdote lead is a brief account of any fact or happening that is amusing. The narrative or anecdote is a lead of action that makes the reader interested and places him/her in an appealing mood.

Example: With a mild atmosphere on Sunday morning, residents in Monrovia and other cities in Sub-Saharan Africa converged in their various churches to commence the celebration of New Year where church bells tolled, and cars with different sirens lined-up between Broad and Ashmun Streets in Monrovia and othermajor streets within Sub-Saharan Africa.

Your Second Paragraph

The second paragraph serves to support and expand on the ideas set out in the lead. It is also a good place to let people know who is "behind" the feature so there will be no confusion about who provided the copy. Also, if the article has to be shortened due to space limitations, having the name of the company or spokesperson and your web address near the beginning will be vitally important. If written well, the first two paragraphs can serve as a brief column item or filler if a newspaper or magazine has only limited space.

Getting into Detail

After the third paragraph, any information you add should develop the story further and hold the interest of the reader. Now is the time to go into detail about the impact of the article, or the mechanisms of how it will affect your reader(s). However, for ease of reading, use bullet points if you are listing information.

CHAPTER FIVE

FINAL TOUCH ON YOUR FEATURE ARTICLE

You WILL NOT WRITE A palatable and appreciable feature story if you forget to reflect on some constituents that could give your feature article the fragrant that will encourage your readers have interest to read your article. These constituents are:

- **Color Piece:** As a feature writer, your story must endeavor to enlighten your audience or readers on a particular theme or subject you are dealing with in your story or article.
- **Behind the Scenes:** Think not of your feature story to shift its focus from the principal event or idea to the background and narrate an interesting tale or fiction.
- **In Disguise:** A feature story that is written while the feature writer is a part of the event. If you are part of the event, you must write in a professional manner that would avail you the opportunity to express your view but yet unsuspected. For instance you want to inject your view without anyone detecting, you write, "it is believed in some quarters that Africa's underdevelopment is mostly due to the non-adherence to democratic tendencies and values". This is a safe escape route for you.

- **Interview:** A feature story that evolves itself around asking questions from respondents or stakeholders, who are usually in a place of prominence is a good sign of a feature writer.

- **How-To:** A good feature story or article is usually dependent on research and helps readers in solving a problem or understanding a scenario.

- **Chronology:** As a feature writer, your feature article or story must strive to provide plain and simple facts mostly in a chronological manner or order.

- **Backgrounder:** If you can briefly reflect on news writing, you will recap the utilization of backgrounding for instance, "it can be recalled that Africa's underdevelopment was discussed by the Heads of Governments at the 10th Summit Meeting held at the African Union Headquarters in Addis Ababa, Ethiopia in 1999". In the same vein, feature story can provide detailed background information relevant to your feature article.

- **Full Texts:** Writing a feature story is not only limited to your interviewees or stakeholders. A full text in this case is nothing but extracts from a book or transcripts obtained during your interview concerning the subject matter of your feature story.

- **Analysis:** A feature writer's story must always analyze the issues or ideas involved an event under report before releasing to the press.

Using Quotes in your feature Article

A quote can lend authority to an article, introduce an expert and further advance the story. Most important, quotes can introduce personal feelings, comments and opinion, so this is where you want to use superlatives and emotive language (without sounding false of course). Be sure quotes are in a conversational style, and do not merely cite facts or figures, no real person speaks only in data. Also avoid repeating information or using jargon; speak as if you were explaining your promotion or achievement to your colleagues on campus. Ideally, the person you quote should be someone who would be available for interviews should another journalist want to ask additional questions. So he or she should be knowledgeable on the topic and open to working with the media. Use your strongest quote first, and be sure to provide information on the speaker and his or her relation to his/her work place in a contact section at the end of your article.

The Use of Images and Multimedia

A photo can often mean a difference between your feature pieces being chosen for publication than choosing your competitor's. A photo helps explain the story and can draw the eye of those scanning the page. It also gives editors more options when filling space.

Make sure your photos are of high-quality: Always provide digital photos in high resolution and if possible, have them shot by a professional if you cannot do it. A bad photo will reflect on the quality of your feature. As you know Africa is within the global communication village, other multimedia options include a video or audio version of your story, or additional expert quotes and interviews. A feature podcast or multimedia news release can include all these assets to transform your story into an online experience for your audience, complete with links and reference materials to let them experience more for themselves.

Releasing Your Feature Article to the Media

Generally, newspaper feature sections are planned long in advance, so you will need to plan ahead. Inform in advance the feature editor to determine their interest before you release your article. If you are trying to get into a trade publication, do your research and check the deadlines; they could be working as much as two to three months in advance.

Most newswires offer feature services and media databases, and they will often offer a feature calendar that corresponds with publications' due dates. Consider distributing your feature via newswire and, if possible, choose one that has a list of when and where your feature could be placed and advises on crafting your feature for the different audiences.

Finally, when sending your feature to editors for publication or editorial consideration, do not be afraid to call them to offer more information; however, do not call to check that the article has arrived. Most feature editors are busy and donot like being bordered or called without good reason. You must therefore be patient, since your feature is not breaking news. The editor may file it for use at the appropriate time at his or her own discretion.

CHAPTER SIX

ETHICS AND FEATURE WRITING

Before PROCEEDING FURTHER, IT IS important to have an understanding of what ethics is when it comes to feature writing. The word ethics is derived from the Greek word ethos which mean custom, habit, character or disposition. Ethics is concerned with what is good for individuals and society. In its simplistic form, ethics is a set of rules that show right or wrong, that is, those principles that guide society to make a positive impact through our decisions and actions.

Ethics play an important role not only in our personal lives, but in our profession, particularly as journalists or mass communicators who will be engaged in feature writing. Most importantly, although ethical issues may concern fraudulent publication, authorship, conflict of interest, but what is more paramount is defamation of character, conflict of interest as a mass communicator.

I am sure you came across defamation of character in news gathering and writing, but just in case it has slipped your mind, defamation of character is putting once character or reputation in public disrepute that is, making someone look ugly in the public eye without any justification.

Consequences of Reporting Feature Article

Remember always that, there are consequences to whatever you do. If you stay in the business long enough you will at a time or another be accused of ruining the reputations of people, businesses, towns or country. If you have the instinct that as a journalist or feature writer you will write your article regardless the consequences, your perception may be right because you cannot afford to let what might happen stand in your way of writing your article on the issue.

But the fact remains that as a feature writer you will not write an article unmindful that there are no consequences. Those squiggles on your notepads and incoherencies on the tape recorder represent the lives of people your article will affect in some way or the other. Therefore, be careful what you write on them.

Facts Versus Truth in Feature Writing

You may not be a student of philosophy, but the issue of fact versus truth is a philosophical one. Nonetheless, the issue is one with relevance to the ethics of feature writing. The issue, more or less, is "What is truth? Its relevance to journalism, particularly feature writing is that there are those who argue that a mere collection of facts, the feature writer habit, does not provide ultimate truth. That could be probably true, since many facts of the moment have needed repair through the years by the truth of history. For example, history may establish that the crises in the African Sub –Region, particularly in Liberian, Sierra Leone, Guinea and other neighboring countries were a demoralizing national mistake.

Yet the facts carried on the media from the inception of those crises seemed to indicate that it was an important pursuit. The problem with truth, unfortunately, is that it comes only with time, time that a feature writer often does not have when writing against the pressure of a deadline. Fortunately, your primary goal is to gather facts, and your responsibility is to get them right.

In the process you record some everlasting truth, so much the better. This point is made not so much to relieve you of the burden of being a diviner of truth, but to warn you against a common beginner's mistake, that of presumption. In the profession of writing, never presume that events will turn out a certain way. For your purposes, the facts of the moment govern. In a sense, you are the public's jury for information, and, like any jury, you cannot convict without evidence. If you try to, you can be sued for distorted and misleading information.

Fairness in Feature Writing

You should always remember that the more relevant concern in feature writing is fairness. Once you enter a working newsroom as a mass communicator or journalist with responsibility to write feature articles, you acquire immeasurable access to one of society's great powers, the power to give or deny you information. You may be an insignificant person of that power. Editors in newsrooms all over, in fact, make the controlling decisions. But you are a part. While objectivity may be one expected ideals, fairness is a responsibility, one that always attends power in a democratic setting or society.

To put fairness in somewhat lofty terms, you are the eyes and ears of the public. How you present a subject is how the public will see it. The public will believe what it see only if it believes you. Moreover, it will believe you only if it trusts what you are saying. As a feature writer, you will deal frequently with matters of controversy and circumstances in which values are in conflict. In order to sustain trust, you must present the issues fairly. When you sit down to write such an article, you should ask yourself simple questions like, "Have I given everybody a fair chance? Have I looked at all of the variables?" Once you have finished the article, you should again ask yourself, "Would I, as a reader, trust this interpretation?" As long as you are satisfied with the answers you derived at, you are good to go.

The Ethical Aspect of Feature Writing

The word 'ethics', according to Felder (2000) comes from the Greek word 'ethos' which means character. Ethics rules are or norms of conduct 'pertaining to the individual character of a person or persons'. Debates on media ethics in Africa have not been theoretically vigorous. In fact, the absence of an established practice of ethical culture has helped the nurturing of media practices where journalists wield enormous power but with minimum responsibility or accountability. Most media institutions have established committees for ethics but yet still the courts get flooded with journalists for ethical transgressions, what a paradox?

Akabogu (2005) notes that ethical transgressions are globally, particularly where Africa seem to be a growing problem. Mass communication experts and professional journalists are generally perceived to be in a position of trust with the society. Any conduct that does not honor and respect the trust put in their professional capacity and integrity could negatively impact the media relationship as well as the professional integrity of the profession at large.

Ethics is the means of knowing the principles regarding what is right and what is wrong within a particular society. That is, the standards that govern the conduct of people, especially members of any organization or profession. If we should reflect on the earlier existence of man, when the children of Israel were in captive for a protracted period of time in Egypt, God commended Moses to go and free them through miraculous powers.

That was accomplished and they were able to cross the Red Sea into the wilderness heading for the promise land. The children were freed but God in His infinite wisdom tried to instill order and homogeneity among them for which He gave the Ten Commandments to Moses to guide the children of Israel while in the wilderness (Exodus 20:1-17).

As a feature writer you must also understand the concept of the *golden rule* which is considered as a law of reciprocity in some religion. This is emphasized in the book of Matthew "Do for others what you want them to do for you that is the meaning of the law of Moses and the teaching of the prophets" (Matthew 7:12)

If you will recall Biblical saying, especially in the Old Testament, or the Hammurabi code you might have heard or read "an eye for an eye". This law is the principle of treating others as one would wish to be treated as the popular saying goes, "what is good for John is good for Paul".

In this regard, your feature article must be void of taking side or writing biased article, favor no one, and deal with the facts and truth. Be objective, balance and credible. Though you may not be a barrister, lawyer, or counselor, as a mass communicator or journalist attempts must be employed to be knowledgeable with the legal and ethical considerations in the profession.

If you may not be aware, every country in this world is guided by the organic law of the country which is the constitution. From the basis of the constitution, media institutions are given direction as to how to operate in line of fairness and balance. Nevertheless, the press in the continent, especially Africa is among the freest in the world. But mind; do not forget about the theories of mass communication which placed a barometer on your scope of reporting depending on the constitution and government, how you report in one country might be different in another country depending on the constitution and tolerance of the government toward the press.

If you find yourself in a country embracing the free flow of information is the brilliance of our forefathers who linked press freedom with the other guaranteed freedom such as religion, right of assembly and speech as well as redress of grievances, though no government can afford to give blanket freedom to its press system, especially where democracy is not flourishing. Understand that as free as the press may be in the African continent, particularly in Sub-Saharan Africa, there are still certain constraints or restrictions and limitations that journalists or mass communicators must be aware of. The most important of these, are the laws pertaining to *defamation of character* and *invasion of privacy.*

I am convinced that this is not your first time coming across the word defamation of character. But for the purpose of this book, defamation of character or calumny, vilification is the transmission or communication of a false statement that impedes or harms the character or reputation of an individual, group, business, nation or government. As a feature writer, you must be mindful how you gather, package and release your information to the press for public consumption so as to avoid being a prey to ethical transgression.

There are two major elements in defamation of character. They are *libel* and *slander.* Libel according to Hopkins (2004) is a false statement about a person that does damage to that person's character or reputation in society. It may cause embarrassment or humiliation, or affect the person's ability to make a living. In libel defamation, the defamer publishes the information for the consumption of the public. This is done mostly in newspapers. For defamation of slander, the defamer uses oral release of the information to the public, through broadcast or oral utterance.

Case Study 2

Your media institution received a tip off through one of your reporters' story concerning an occurrence of a flood in the capital city and the ministry or agency responsible to remedy the situation received some huge sum of money to contain the flood since the lives and properties of dwellers are affected. The incidence is of human interest and your media institution decides to write a feature story on the situation, but then, your institution failed to verify or contact the relevant stakeholders of the ministry or agency mentioned because you relied on your reporter's report. The key issue is huge sum of money is involved to combat the flood and you decides to write a feature article on the incidence. In your feature write – up, your analysis mentioned the ministry or agency for squandering the money to the detriment of the city dwellers that got gravely affected by the flood. It happened that the information is not true since no money was released to any ministry or agency to remedy to flood situation. Indeed, plans were being made by the government through the Ministry of Finance to make money available to the ministry or agency responsible to contain the flood, and your reporter did not get this fact but rather decided to write the article without authentication. Your feature article is published in your newspaper and posted on the newsstand with the minister of the ministry or agency concerned to remedy the flood name mentioned placing him or her in public disrepute.(How do you see this, will your media institution not be held responsible for ethical transgression)? If not, why?

Perkins(2003) notes that invasion of privacy is the intrusion into the Personal life of another without just cause --this can give the person whose privacy has been invaded the right to bring a lawsuit for damages against the person that intruded. In short, Perkins (2003) is noting that invasion of privacy is the unjustifiable intrusion into the personal life of another without consent. This situation can be considered a tort or wrongful act which can be punishable through legal action against the perpetrator.

CHAPTER SEVEN

EDITORIAL WRITING

An EDITORIAL IS A LEADING article written by senior editorial people or publisher of a newspaper, magazine or any other written journalistic document most of the time not signed or with no by - line. In its generality, editorial deals with every day or recent events and happenings that strives to contrive viewpoints based on an objective analysis of issues and conflicting or contrary opinions. Editorial is an article that presents the newspaper's position or view on an issue of relevance to society. It reflects the majority role of the editorial board, the governing body of the media entity made up of editors, senior reporter, and the business department or managers.

As you journey through this chapter, let it be understood that the purpose of any editorial globally is to tackle immediate occurrences or events of society and strive to formulate the viewpoints of those involved not divorced from objective analysis of events and conflicting or varied opinions or views. Note that all editorials are predominantly concerned about balance and objectivity. Also, it must be understood that every editorial matters are more related to the content of a particular issue rather than its commercial benefit. Most importantly, editorial is one of the important ways to share the media's entity position of how it sees things or advocate for a course in society.

Bear in mind that as you join the team to write editorials, the audience will under – appreciate your editorial piece because it will not have your by-line or name of anybody (writer). Notwithstanding, the importance of editorial cannot be over emphasized because a separate column, page or sections are always allocated in every edition or publication of the newspaper or magazine just for editorial. This avails your news entity the opportunity to communicate or express to your audience or reader an opinion or view you share and feel is of importance for society.

What is Editorial?

As we attempt to define editorial, it will be good to make an analogy with a lawyer or counselor and editorial. The function of a lawyer or counselor is to build an argument, defend and persuade to court through the presiding judge to buy his or her argument or think the same way. This is just what editorial is all about, the only difference is the lawyer or counselor is confined to a specific locale which is the court and editorial is operated in the court of public opinion.

Editorial in the real sense or by way of definition, is the unified or corporate voice or stand of any operative media institution on any given issue affecting the interest of the public. In its simplistic form, editorial or leader is the opinion or mouth piece of the newspaper or any other media entity engaged in the dissemination of information, *particularly news gathering and reporting*. Most importantly LaRocque (2003) notes that editorials are written for the understanding of readers to intrigue them to take or make prompt decisions to effectuate a change on the particular issue reported in the newspaper. You might want to know the word *leader* in editorial. Leader in this case refers to the leading role plaid in informing society on issues that shape the destiny of people to make them take the appropriate decision or action which is the editorial.

Duyile (2005) notes that an editorial is an explanatory writing or opinion of the newspaper on any topic and further noted that editorial is a comment or an argument in support of a particular policy, an action, or an idea whether expressed or latent. It can be an argument exhibiting the logical reasoning of the newspaper using the thoughts of the proprietor for the purpose of persuading the readers or audience to kick against an idea, policy or an action based on facts available (Duyile, 2005).

As in the fundamental purpose and objective of journalism or mass communication, editorial serves as a critical assessment interpretation of information on topical issues aimed at informing, educating and entertaining the readers. In most instances, editorials explain issues or persuade target readers especially stakeholders to take action. Throwing more light on the issue of editorial or leader, Duyile (2005) further described editorial as an explanatory text or the opinion of the newspaper concerning any contemporary topic or issue that will affect the lives of people. In summation, editorials are write-ups in the media, especially newspapers that give the media's opinion about something rather than objective reporting which is based on facts that are not divorced from the elements of straight news writing.

The Origin of Editorial

Yassa (1996) recounts the origin of editorial can be traced as far back as 1830 when the term editorial was used as a label to designate a statement of the editor's opinion. The word editorial was used then to refer to an article written by the editor. However, in contemporary times the posture of editorial has evolved to a larger extent where newspaper the world over had designated a separate editorial column or page for editorials.

It is important to note that with the advancement of technology, modern newspapers have tremendously expanded and enriched the editorial pages to the point that it is been used to face lengthier expression of opinions.

In his description, Ukonu (2005) notes that editorial is the melting pot for all kinds of journalistic writings. According to the author, investigative, interpretative and hard news reporting are incorporated into editorials (Ukonu, 2005). The author Ukonu (2005) furthered that objectivity, precision, speculation and advocacy are also styles adopted in treating editorial writings and because of the melting pot posture of an editorial, it can be argued that its components are drawn from the components of other journalistic articles.

Editorial Versus News Writing

Editorial as discussed in its definition is the corporate opinion of the media entity on given issues of public interest. In this direction, making an analysis between editorial and news writing, news writing deals with *objective* materials while editorial pieces deal with *subjective* materials. Editorials can captivate public interest or opinion either in favor or against topical issues of relevance. News is all about the recounting of current events that make people cope with happenings in their environment. News reports are greatly influenced by events or activities and people. As you may have come across the factors that are determinants of news writing, it is necessary to do a recap for better understanding.

These factors are:

- Proximity
- Timeliness
- Consequences
- Prominence
- Oddities
- Human interest

It is quite obvious that you went through the rudiments of the above listed factors in basic news writing, however, I will endeavor to do refresher for the sake of academic expediency.

Proximity – Commonly known as propinquity means closeness or nearness in space. Residents in Accra, Lagos, Free Town, or Monrovia for instance would be concerned about a shortage of food in those capital cities when there is surplus of food in other cities far from them. Or yet still, people will be more interested in what affect them directly than what affects other people of distance even though they are in the same country or continent.

Timeliness – This is most of the time referred to as immediacy. Immediacy in an event means closeness in time. An event that occurred

RICHMOND S. ANDERSON, SNR.

last week for instance, is less newsworthy than an event of the same magnitude that happened last night because of the time duration or interval.

Consequences – There is gainsaying the fact that the audience or reader always takes interest in events that have implications or effects on their lives, both now and in the future. It will be easier for people's interest to be generated when there is an abrupt increase in the price of transportation due to fuel shortage in the country. Such a situation will claim the attention of readers or audience any time it is reported in the news.

Prominence – It is an acceptable fact that big people, big events make instance news. Big shots such as presidents, legislators, parliamentarians, and prelates in any society make news in what they do and say. As a student are you prominent? **Oddities**- News can be weird and bizarre depending on its occurrence. Odd happenings like war, natural disasters, coup d' etats among others often attract screaming headlines in most newspapers and magazines. Oddities are news about the bad, the odd and the ugly.

Human Interest – Some events are news worthy because they make the average reader to empathize with the victims. Events like deaths, armed robbery and accidents have human interest nuances because they can happen to anybody. Straight forward news reporting or factual news is a kind of report that says it as it is. News reports provide platform for features and editorial writing. Before any editorial can be written on issue, it must first of all be reported by way of news either for the electronic or print media. It is therefore the job or responsibility of the editorial staff to interpret the news, analyze it and advance public opinion on crucial matters from the news.

Editorial Versus Feature

No matter what you think, editorial writing is purely research oriented. It is something applicable to feature writing. A feature is a *creative* journalistic writing which strives to inform, explain, analyze, and interpret issues in the interest of the readers. Awoyinfa & Igwe (1991:5) state feature is a colorful story about people, events, places and life. It is written in an interesting and creative manner with information drawn from people involved, eyewitnesses, experts on the subjects and those affected by the subject. As implied by their status, features and editorials provide for deeper and logical analysis of issues.

According to Okoro & Agbo (2003:96), there is a dichotomy between features and editorials in the following ways:

o Most features carry bylines, that is, they are assigned by their writers.
o Usually editorials do not carry bylines.
o Features can be accompanied illustrations. In most cases, editorials are not illustrated (no photographic illustrations)
o Features are usually the result of individual efforts, while editorials are the result of group effort, that is, the editorial board.

Characteristics of Editorial

Just as in news writing where you have to get information from a source that is the same way process in editorial writing. No editorial can just emerge from the blue sky. All editorial materials have news nuances. It must be a topical issue that has been reported in the mass media either in the print or electronic by way of hard news or features. Such an issue must attract the attention of the public and generate debate.

On this premise, it is safe to note that an editorial is comprised of news and feature elements. In giving an analysis, an editorial also has some features of anews story because of its subjectivity posture. In affirmation Ate (2006) notes that in some cases, thought-provoking letters to the editor are often used to gauge public opinion and when critically utilized, letters to the editor could serve as useful raw materials in writing an editorial. This is because letters to the editor can give useful insights into emerging controversial and topical issues of public significance (Ate, 2006).

In short, editorial components are drawn from other journalistic sources or write-ups. No matter the status of the media institution, an editorial carries an institutional flavor. That is why in writing an editorial, the usage of "we" or the name of the newspaper is most of the time used rather than "I" or the name of the writer of the editorial. Editorial is an organizational affairs and therefore all credits or blames accruing from it must go to the institution or organization and not an individual.

What is a Good Editorial?

As an editorial writer, it is important to know some hints guiding the idea of editorial writing. Below are some editorial writing hints:

- As stated earlier, an editorial must have an institutional flavor. It is the media institution that should be heard speaking in an editorial not a person or individual.
- In order to accomplish the mission of an editorial, the language of the editorial should be plain and unambiguous. No matter what the editorial is intended for, the language must be understood by the target audience.
- In writing an editorial, you should always be exact. Say what you want to say without meandering *(beating about the bush)*. Do not create room for verbosity.
- Since you are writing in the interest of people on issues affecting them, your editorial must be rich in human interest. You believe it or not, people are interested in the affairs of their fellow humans. Even though your writing is geared towards expressing the opinion analytically, your editorial must always be catchy and attention grabbing. Dull and weak editorials cannot create the desired impact on its target readers or audience.
- Originality is the hall mark in editorial writing. Every editorial must be original in tone and substance. A media institution, especially newspaper entity should not engage in the habit of dubbing or cut and pasting another paper's editorial in the name of being voguish.

- Just as in any scholastic work of which you cannot leave out feature, research plays a pivotal role in editorial writing. Editorial must be well researched to give you an appreciable piece that would be acclaimed by the reader. Newspapers should factor timeliness into qualitative and quantitative research if an editorial masterpiece is to be produced.
- News writing and feature stories are written based on facts. Equally so, editorials must be written based on facts, not speculations. Credibility must be a fulcrum of your opinion piece.

Above all, an editorial is distinctively unique because of the institutional garment it wears. That makes an editorial a powerful weapon in shaping public opinion.

Types of Editorial

Just as in essay writing where you have the different forms of essay, editorial writing is a concept that deals with case presentation that has different approaches and types. Basically there are six types of editorials according to my reading, they include the below stated:

- Editorial of Information or Explanation
- Editorial of Interpretation
- Editorial of Criticism
- Editorial of Commendation,
- Editorial of Argumentation
- Editorial of Entertainment

Editorial of Information/Explanation – This editorial seeks to give information on facts of news stories or add fact with minimum explanation. It may define terms, identify persons or factors, or provide a background. Additionally editorial of information or explanation strives to present the burning issues unfolding in society for the judgment of the readers. They are thought-provoking issues of concern which generate the interest of the reader and provide the space for them to judge. They may also create room to identify problem, explain same and make readers to explore for solution.

Editorial of Interpretation – Interpretative editorial explains the significance or meaning of a news event, current ideas, condition, or situation, theory, or hypothesis. The writer doesn't argue nor criticize, but merely present both sides of an issue and leaves the judgment to the reader. It merely interprets, say for example, the conduct of a new memorandum issued by the president or chancellor of the university regarding students stand off on campus. Interpretative editorials are mainly written for purpose or mission aimed at explaining issues of major concern and placing facts and figures to cause readers for illumination of the day's issue. Depending on the issue, interpretative editorials could be positive or negative and even neutral in posture depending on the circumstance and angle that the writer will focus on the subject matter or issue. **Editorial of criticism–** This editorial points out the good or the bad features of a problem or situation mentioned in the news. Its purpose is to influence the reader. It suggests a solution at the end. Criticism editorials are written with a specific mission to send out a particular point on the issue being dealt with. Such editorials strive to convince the reader on the importance or inevitability of a particular issue while pointing the opposite side in bad light.

In criticism editorials, there is no place for neutrality and can strongly oppose a cause or wholeheartedly support the issue.

Editorial of Commendation, Appreciation, or Tribute – This editorial praises, commends, or pays tribute to a person or organization that has performed some worthwhile projects or deeds, or accomplishments.

Editorial of Argumentation - This is oftentimes called editorial of persuasion. The editor argues in order to convince or persuade the audience or reader to accept his/her stand on the issue propounded.

Editorial of Entertainment– This editorial evokes a smile, a chuckle, laughter, while suggesting truth. Its main aim is to entertain, but with a message as the cardinal focus.

Editorial of Mood – Mood editorial presents a philosophy rather than an argument or explanation. Oftentimes, the subject matter is nature or emotion.

Where to Source Editorial Materials?

In basic straight news writing, news items are sourced from what is called *news beat* that is, places, entities or organizations where reporters are assigned to fetch for news materials to be written into news stories. For editorials, the sourcing of the materials can mainly be obtained from current events that are reported in the media. As complexities are becoming more glaring on our global village, especially with the emergence of social media, editorials can be sourced from the internet in a computer demanded society. Computers in such a case can be browsed by the media institution to get materials of relevance to the editorial issue relevant to society.

You often hear of secondary materials or sources. Such is the case in editorial writing. It is worth noting that multiple of records are available documenting activities of society, be it good or bad. Editorial writers can easily reach out to such documents since they are printed and public records are intended for public consumption. Such records can be books, journals, government documents such as gazette, taxes, assembly or legislative proceedings, and even constitutions.

It is undeniable that most of us do not attend social gatherings or functions where social interactions take place. Journalists, especially members of the editorial board are not supposed to be social novice. They must be able to possess the virtue of human relations and mingle with people of different classes in order to get insight into the happenings in their environs. Going to conferences, and parties with prominent people or big shots in society would help greatly to understand the posture that would aid the editorialists to derive at good analysis concerning the people they meet.

As editorial writer, it is important to be familiar with law enforcement officers. Additional information can be obtained from them regarding any issue under probe. Above all, in editorial writing, a thorough and comprehensive research is needed to interpret or analyze a news phenomenon from the perspective of an editorial. Understand that editorials are research oriented and effort must be put in place by the editorial staff in eliciting information or data for the sake of writing the editorial. A good editorial staff must be a body of robustness socially literate among other factors for the cultivation of credible sources for the editorial piece or article.

How to Detect Editorial Materials?

It is now clear that you have to solicit editorial materials from relevant sources. After the materials, the editorial board or designate writer has to make sure that they are relevant, rich or not. In this direction, Duyile (2005) made the following identification of testing editorial materials process up to the final writing of the editorial. You must give the editorial material a rigid test by reading them thoroughly over and over and understand from what materials to be utilized. He furthered that you write down first, the main points, and the facts of the topic before considering what comment to add.

Editorial writers must always check their points and facts collected from the materials before writing the real editorial. As a journalist, you are not precluded from observing the professional ethics in editorial writing. You must at all times be within the confines of professional ethics, especially when it comes to demonstrating your editorial judgment and suggestions.

In the process of writing your editorial, you must be precise and concise in giving background information which in most cases must precede or come before the body of the editorial. Apart from the introduction portion of the editorial, all references must be treated in brief. In editorial writing, there is no rambling or beating around the bush. Go straight to the point you are dealing with. Observe word economy, that is, do not be wordy. Make sure you don't leave your readers or audience in oblivion on your stand on the issue under discussion.

Furthermore, in writing an editorial, you must be exact. Write what you want to write without merry go rounding or beating round the bush. There should be no room for verbosity. Journalistic writings are most of the time centered on human interest. Therefore, your editorial must be rich in human interest. This is because people are interested in the affairs of their fellow human beings. An editorial or leader must be catchy and attention grabbing. Weak and dull editorials cannot create the desire impact on its readers or target audience. Persuasive techniques and other appeals can be used for this purpose.

Originality in the tone of editorial writing is cardinal. It is not advisable to dub other papers' editorial in the name of being superficial.

As we have repeatedly stressed on the importance of research, an editorial must be researched. Media institutions should factor timeliness into qualitative and quantitative research if an editorial master piece is to be produced.

Things to Know When Writing Editorial

Just as in other composition or essay writings, editorials are not written from a vacuum. There must be an interesting issue of public concern that needs to be treated as per the target readers or audience. To write an appreciable editorial is one of a difficult task. It is task that calls for commitment, diligence, and originality. Getting your editorial materials alone is not sufficient bases for writing a good editorial. As an editorial writer you must be sound and logical in your presentation. Always make sure that your editorial topics are of current events or contemporary issues and must be weighty in expressing direction toward the socio-political and economic worth of society.

Arguments propounded in editorial writing must be valid and authoritative in tone, and of course not divorced from the editorial policy of the media institution. Discipline is one of the cardinal hall marks in writing an editorial, particularly in the choice of words. No matter the variation of the audience, the language in the editorial must be more of patronizing. No matter how you take it, there is no space or time for excess use of words and circumlocution as they will only hinder the quality of the message. Be simple in the choice of words and to the point the editorial is hammering.

As an editorial writer you must be proactive to always write and rewrite, revise your script or article and do some substantive editing of your article. Just as in essay writing, you must remember that there are three elements in editorial writing. They include, the introduction, the purpose which is the body in essay writing, and the closing which is the conclusion in essay writing. Let us journey on journey on brief highlights of these elements for your utilization as you attempt to write an editorial piece.

The Introduction – If your editorial must be of attention – grabbing, you must start it with a the introduction with an unusual or unique and catchy, question, statistic, quotation, or any piecing sentence relevant to your topic that will serve as a catalyst to lured the reader to your article. You must know that you are, as an editorial writer in the court of public opinion therefore, you must present your argument at this stage of your article.

The Purpose – First ask the question, what is the purpose of my editorial? It is at this stage your editorial article should explain your idea or issue you dealing with objectively. Please do not involve any biasness as you endeavor to explain the issue. Do not leave any stone unturned, explain and discuss each and every aspect of the topic you dealing with, this is where you make use of the "who, why, where, when, and what" of course, not leaving out the "how". You can start by addressing your readers or audiences who might have counter view to your issue. To win them over, you can even highlight the positive side of the opposition as long as they are factual. If you find it expedient, you can refute the opposing side and provide strong reasons and tangible evidence that will help with the credibility of your position. When you are addressing the problem in your editorial, you must project or propose a valid and relevant solution for the problem.

The Conclusion – In your conclusion, always strive to end your editorial with a strong or powerful thought – provoking statement that would warrant the reader's attention as this will give your readers a sense of closure.

Editorial and its Audience

In mass communication which is a conglomerate of the various media outlets, you will always find a diversified of target groups and audience. Editorials are no exception, you communicate in editorials therefore they must have target audience depending on the issue your editorial is analyzing. In this connection, editorial write – ups have three major audience to grapple with. If these audiences are fully understood, it will guide the editorial writer to hit the target by giving the right message. If you know your audience as editorial writer, you will avoid a void target thereby making your editorial more effective and rewarding.

As you may be aware, life itself is dynamic; so is communication depending on what you want to communicate. In editorial writing, there are three types of editorial audiences. They are:

✓ The selective audience
✓ The skeptical audience
✓ The obstinate audience

In examining the three audiences, Ate (2006) stated that the selective audience, are specialized audience who care only about what goes on in their chosen fields. They are addicted to the knowledge in their fields or disciplines and are glued to same without bothering about things outside their areas of interest. For instance if your editorial pin on professions like medicine, agriculture, or computer science, your audience already targeted in the professions listed will only be interested in their areas of specialty.

In furtherance Ate (2006) noted that the skeptical audience is sophisticated audience with high aura of excellence. These are people who question everything including facts, figures, grammar, tone, style and content of every editorial until they are satisfied. They are the educated and curious people who are conscious of their fundamental human rights. As an editorial writer, you must always recognize this group of audience and direct your editorial to meet their demand and standard. For the obstinate audience Ate (2006) noted that this group of people is blind critics. You must write your editorial that goes their way.

Anything said or written outside their frame of reference by someone else is completely wrong. They are limited in their thinking and analysis. They often feed on rumor mongering. They are intellectual lumped who believe that holding an opinion is a transgression against public order.

Who is an Editorial Writer?

Editorial is not the personal activity by an individual. As stated earlier, it is a corporate venture that propels the voice of the entity. But by consensus of the establishment or the editorial board someone can be designated to write editorial pieces. With this in mind, an editorial writer can be classified as a professional journalist or mass communicator that knows the issues and able to compose in a journalistic form expressing the opinion of the media entity. In every media establishment, especially newspapers, a group of knowledgeable writers referred to as editorial board members are clothed with the responsibility of writing editorials. This responsibility is solely delegated to the composer by the editorial board which usually has a chairman. In most cases, the editorial board is composed of people of different intellectual backgrounds or some of the writers pooled from various professions. Depending on the media setting and country editorial board members can be internal or external. For instance a comparative analysis of the population and media landscape of the Federal Republic of Nigeria and the Republic of Ghana cannot be equated to that of the population of Liberia, Sierra Leone, or the Gambia who have smaller population.

It must be understood that topics for editorial writing are selected at board meetings and endorsed with acquiesce of board members. The editorial board also serves as the formulators of policies for the media institution. Whatever direction the media institution takes in terms of reportage must be guided by the editorial board which is the decision making body.

In most cases, some media institutions do not have laid down policies that would provide guidance and the trend of their reportage. Editorial board members usually meet, select and discuss topical editorial issues. The editorial board of any media institution must be of men and women of intelligence, sound educational acumen or background and social ability to interact with every strata of society. They are people who possess the pedigreed to make sound and logical analysis on topical issues.

Case Study 3

Your media institution is established newly and there is no editorial board to lead or direct the institution in writing an editorial. You all are editors, reporters and the newsroom is functional with reporters assigned to the various news beats with no limitation on what kind of news to gather and report. Your newspaper is published and an editorial is emanated from one of the stories, but then the newsroom is not guided by editorial policies and orientations, editorial credibility, editorial appeal, news peg, editorial contact, editorial integrity and editorial calendar. Suppose the issue you reported in your editorial is detrimental to the security of the state unknowingly. If you have check list of what your media institution should report and what not to report, you will detect that the editorial article will be directed at another issue rather than that of the security implication. With this determination, you will save your institution from getting into problem with the state.

Editorial writing is cumbersome and it cannot be tagged to just anybody. In this regard, those editorial writers assigned the task must possess some attributes that will make them stand up to the task. To be a radio broadcaster or an essayist you must have the mastery of language, good knowledge and writing skills and good pronunciation. It is almost the same trend in editorial writing, except that as editorial writer, you must be intellectually alert, your issues must be logical and meticulous *(care for details)* and of course, have an analytical mind.

It is important to know that editorial policy is the beliefs of a media institution which it would like to manifest in its news coverage. In another form, editorial policy is a definite course of action selected from among alternatives to guide and shape present and future actions. For your editorial to have the required impact on the targeted readers, it must be well written and be rich in substance, tone and style.

Editorial Writing Techniques

No matter what your intension is in writing an editorial, most editorials are aimed at winning the affection of the readers. We all perceive things differently based on our socio-cultural differences. What you may see as white, may be seen as gray by someone else. In this direction, for you the editorial writer to be able toconvince readers to go along with your view, the editorial must contain reasonable pieces of persuasion. Persuasion plays an important role in editorial writing. (*You must be able to convince your readers*).

Relationship between Research and Editorial

Research, by now should not be a strange phenomenon to you because in your earlier reading, you were told that it is the means of conducting an inquiry on what you already know or what you don't know. Notwithstanding, for further knowledge, research can be considered as the systematic collection and interpretation of information to increase the understanding of your readers or audience. As editorial writer, you must acquire enough accurate, relevant data onthe issue you trying to project in the interest of the consumers of the message or readers.

An editorial cannot be divorced from news and feature elements. In sourcing for editorial materials, such synergy must be considered. In this regard, in writing an editorial, a thorough research is needed to analyze or interpret a news event from the perspective of an editorial. Just as in feature writing, editorials are research oriented and therefore many efforts must be exerted in eliciting the relevant data as editorial writer. A good editorial writer must be a field person and socially inclined to source credible information for an editorial piece.

The Importance of Research in Editorial Writing

In any critical writing, especially editorial, research is the most focal point. Regardless of your professional orientation, no journalist can write a good editorial on any topical issue of the day unless authentic facts or data are on hand which can only be acquired through research. In basic news writing, if you are to reflect on a little bit of historicity, you will need to do back grounding by stating your reference like "it can be recalled that…" Also in editorial writing, you deal with a deeper back grounding on issue you want to editorialize on in a different dimension as compared to that of the basic news. To achieve this goal, you must formulate different ways of getting the necessary data before writing. Suppose you want to write an editorial on an eminent person's achievement in society, it will be an impossible venture if you do not know the relevant information on the person. Equally so, it is impossible for editorial writers to write a good editorial on any issue without a clear understanding on the intricacies that led to the emergence in the news event reported. It is only through research these intricacies can be thoroughly understood. It is not intentioned to bore you much with research methodologies since you are not presently engaged in thesis or research writing. However, it is important to have a glimpse on the different types of research as it will help you to determine what kind of research you might want to employ while writing your editorial piece.

For the purpose of the subject under discussion, the below research methods can be used to add color to your editorial back grounding:

- ➤ Descriptive research
- ➤ Historical research
- ➤ Survey research
- ➤ Field research

It is important that you add value to your reading of this book, particularly students, do more reading on the above listed research methods. It will greatly help build your intellectual horizon.

CHAPTER EIGHT

PUBLIC OPINION AND EDITORIAL

THE COHESIVENESS AND CONGENIALITY OF society to some degree, depend on public opinion, especially when it comes to political activities. Political activities in an appreciable democratic sphere have the ability to enhance the distribution of opinions on a wide range of issues aimed at exploring the impact of special interest groups on election outcomes. These activities also have the ability to contribute to societal knowledge about the effects of government propaganda and policy most of the time facilitated editorial write - ups.

Since it is perceive that public opinion can undeniably be influenced by publication and the political media, editorials are pivotal for the realization of this task. The media, particularly editorials have the power to influence beliefs, attitudes, and behaviors of people and their environment for the advancement of society. In any social setting, information is abundantly necessary because it creates common knowledge of a norm and enhance social interaction and coordination as individuals move readily accept the information if they are convinced that others have also accept same, that is the information. The influence therefore of the mass media particularly editorials have great impact on many aspects of human existence, especially during lectionary period.

What is Public Opinion?

Public opinion is the homogeneous or collective views of members of the society concerning a particular issue. Harrower (2007) noted that public opinion is a multiplicity of the views and feelings of the public on contemporary and pertinent issues of concern and of significance to the people. The issue could be economic, political or social. Take for instance, the capture of the Chibok girls by Boko Haram in Nigeria, the 2017 run-off elections in Liberia, and the 2018 run-off elections in Sierra Leone. These issues were center of discussion not only in those countries of occurrences, but also in the global community because of their relevance to global politics and human interest.

The Structure of Public Opinion

Public opinion as defined above, can be understood as consisting of the desires, wants, and thinking of the majority of the people -- thereby leading to the collective opinion of people of any given society or state on an issue or problem. In primordial era, Bernays & Miller (2005) noted that society was not at its peak of consciousness and enlightenment. Almost every body in a society or state paid homage to the chief, king, or authority that the people depended upon for direction. As society began to advance with the saturation of civilization, people's mind started advancing and philosophers evolved and concepts were designed to suit society. From historical perspective, with the emergence of philosophers, the concept of public opinion came about through the process of urbanization and other political and social forces (Bernays & Miller,2005).

In addition, Barker (1996) mentioned that numerous theories and substantial evidence exist to lay the basis for the structure and dynamics of individuals' opinions. Most of this research draws on psychological studies on people's attitudes, especially in communication studies and political science, mass media which are often considered as influential forces on public opinion. Berner(1996) further notes that research is a political socialization and behavioral genetics which sometimes highlight public opinion.

Structurally, public opinion starts with agenda setting by major media institutions throughout the world. This agenda setting dictates what is newsworthy and how and when it will be reported. Another key component in the structural formation of public opinion is framing. Framing is all about news portrayal in a particular way and is meant to sway the consumer's or audience attitude one way or the other (Lewis, 2003).

Social desirability is another key component to the structural formation of public opinion. Social desirability according to Lewis (1992) is the ideas that people in general will form their opinions based on what they believe is the prevalent opinion of the social group they identify with. Based on media agenda setting and media framing, most often a particular opinion gets repeated throughout various news media.

Editorial Versus Public opinion

It is clear that the mass media, be it in the Western or African setting has been playing and continue to play a cardinal role in the shaping of public opinion. In fact, the focal role of the mass media is the formation of public opinion that resulted to the *fourth estate* to be titled the court of public opinion. The court of public opinion is where issues that revolve around the interest of public opinion and its formation are examined or discussed by the ordinary people at different levels of strata (Arnold, 2003).

You have often been told about the fourth estate as the fourth branch of government not being paid directly from tax payers' money. It is important that you get an insight on the fourth estate, especially its origin. Breger (2015) notes that although there are many individuals such as Thomas Carlye and Edmund Burke in the 1700s who were credited to have originally used the terminology fourth estate, on March 26, 2017 they attributed the term fourth estate to Lord Brougham who used the term in 1823. Others such as the three estates preceding the fourth estate were the King, the Clergy and the Commoners(Mills, 2005).

In the American political system Mills (2005) asserted that the unofficial fourth branch of government was to a group that influences the other three branches of the United States Federal Government that was defined in the American constitution (Legislature, Executive and Judiciary) -- such groups can include the press (an analogy for the fourth estate). The concept of the media or press as a fourth branch therefore stems from a belief that the news media's responsibility to inform the populace is essential to the healthy functioning of a democratic society.

The Usefulness of Public Opinion

It is unarguable that the mass media is indisputably the mouth piece of the society. Society has expanded through population explosion which has caused the aggressiveness expansion of people in society. Notwithstanding, the mass media remains the only sure voice where people will express their voice, opinions, and views. The usefulness of public opinion can be expressed in the following ways:

➢ Public opinion provides the resources for determining the posture or image of an organization or individual. Practically, if an individual wanting to run for a public office in parliament or legislature his/her popularity can be measured by public opinion if he/she so desire.

➢ Public opinion reveals the need for social change which is the basis for the transformation of society.

➢ The mass media keeps eye on issues and predicts the future prospect of any organization.

➢ Public opinion provides the basis for research through exposing some pertinent areas that would generate public debate.

➢ Good governance is the expectation of a healthy democracy. Hence, public opinion creates the forum for the formulation of policy and planning for any willing government.

➢ There is an adage that says nothing is permanent except change. The mass media or a mass communicator through his or her interaction with various members of the society is an agent of change. The journalist or mass communicator keeps a tab on human and organization behaviors and in line with public position or opinion may champion the course of social change in a society. If editorial is put in the proper perspective, its appearance in the local dailies in Africa will predict financial and developmental future of the continent. The mass media will keep its watchful eye on a particular organization and predict the organization's future financial status through the help of public opinion.

➤ Public opinion as a component of the mass media sets agenda for the society. One of the major functions of the press is to set agenda for the good governance of the society. The journalist without getting in touch with the views of members of the society cannot set any effective agenda.

Acknowledging the agenda setting power of the media Cohen (1963) noted that the media may not be successful most of the time in telling people what to think, but they are stunningly successful in telling them what to think about. The ability of the media to determine public thinking is an agenda setting exercise. In his view Daramola (2003) stated that when the press seizes a great issue to thrust unto the agenda of talk, it moves action on it. That underscores the importance of the agenda setting functions of the press which is only made possible through public opinion. It is worth noting that public opinion can be determined through elections, referendum, opinion polls and having meetings with people.

Derivation of Public Opinion

Barrage of issues are conduit for the formation of public opinion. However, there are some other ways public opinion can be derived. Some of the ways are:

- As you know the radio, television, newspapers and magazines are all channels of communication where people express their views. Therefore, the mass media is a conglomerate to formulate public opinion.

- Political parties and other organizations such as pressure groups can serve as creation for the formulation of public opinion.
- Public opinion can also be formulated through peer groups, especially among youths in organizations with shared values and influences.
- Public opinion can be further derived from symposia and lectures as they provide avenues for brainstorming on ideas whose molecules can be used in constructing public opinion. Also, we can derived at public opinion based on people's orientation or background who, by geographical, professional or social background can expose them to public issues or debates to serve as useful resource in the formation of public opinion.

Commonality Between Opinion and Editorial

There is a strong relationship between public opinion and editorial pieces. Issues discussed in the mass media may start at insignificant level but will later burst into public awareness. At this level the editorial writer takes a stance to either go for or against the burning issue in the court of public opinion. Editorials all over the world perform specific functions and they include though not limited to the below stated:

- ❖ Editorials throw more light (illuminate) on issues of the day by looking at the two sides of a particular issue.
- ❖ Editorials bring to focus issues that are debatable and provide the platform for an intellectual view for society to discuss aimed at economic, political and moral quandaries.
- ❖ Regardless of societal status, editorials most often defend the less privilege and underdogs in society. It is a fact that in any society there always exist different dimensions of natural and artificial, political and economic gaps between the haves and the haves not, the powerful and the powerless, the educated and the uneducated.
- ❖ As an opinion oriented writing, editorials appeal or persuade the readers to accept right or wrong things of the issue under spotlight.

❖ Editorials endorse or support an issue of public significance. On this note, editorialists should know that they are dogmatic set of barking and biting professionals, whose stock in trade to only attack. Editorials can also support noble causes of the public concern. For instance, any time policy makers and executors are on the right track, some editorials acknowledge their efforts.

In supporting or endorsing their policy, there might be some grey areas where the supportive editorials may call for fine-turning. The essence of good written editorials is to have impact on society. As stated earlier, good editorials most of the time galvanizes policy formulation on the part of government and concerned stakeholders for the advancement of society.

In a more detailed manner, editorials indicate, inform and create a stage to entertain the public on wide range of issues in the society. Society as you may know is interwoven through people's interactions. In view of this, editorials can create a pathway for parliamentarians or legislators to initiate bills or laws that would eventually represent the voice of the society.

An impact creating editorial must truly represent the hopes and aspirations of the people. In its posture or form, editorials perform powerful opinion functions in the mass media. In this regard, it empowers the mass media to function as one of the leading forces in the formation of public opinion.

CHAPTER NINE

PERSUASION AND EDITORIAL WRITING

IN ANY EMERGING DEMOCRATIC SOCIETY like Africa, the media and persuasion which are inter woven particularly in the area of editorial writing have a composite relation with germ of power and any political system. In this direction, both always emit information and attitudes neutral from government and interest of power. Furthermore, in pursuit of persuasion and disseminating information, those with interest promote news and information closely connected to political parties and other concerned groups. Based on this symbiotic mutuality, there is always a close relation between the media and politics, especially when persuasion becomes a dominant issue.

Persuasion and editorial pieces always strive to convince its readers or audiences of certain belief that usually leads to taking an action. This is why persuasion skills are of vital importance since they help portray professionals and your readers to change preconceived notions of their potential clients and make them believe in what is released to them. The ability to persuade your readers is to understand their needs and expectations based on the situation and be able to address them will be an effective way of persuasion – cause them to believe in you.

What is Persuasion?

Persuasion is the act of trying to advancing of arguments to someone or reader(s) with the intention of changing their mind or convincing them on a certain point of view or course of action. In their views Weaver & Hybels (2001) persuasion is a process that occurs when the communicator (sender) influences the values, beliefs and attitudes or behaviors of another person (receiver). Based on this definition, it can be construed that persuasion is a planned and deliberate effort by the writer or communicator to get his point of view patronized or accepted by his target audience.

It is a soul-searching venture that results to get other people to accept one's position on an issue or any subject matter. If you are to cajole or convince your readers, the editorial must put across a well-articulated and reasoned argument and provide incontrovertible information. Resonating the great philosopher Aristotle, when rhetoric and public speaking where on the high scale, he perceived the idea of persuasion as a masterstroke in the game of communication. For him, communication has three components, including the speaker, the speech and the receiver or audience.

The Role of Persuasion in Editorial Writing

Editorial writing which requires analytical thinking is not a congruent style of thinking. That is, each individual has their own style of analytical thinking. This is not to say that analytical thinking does not follow rules or standards, but rather, that each person thinks and analyze things differently. This is fine, so long as the basic tenets of analytical thinking, arguments, and reasoning are followed and met. One way analytical thinking difference may be apparent is when an individual engaging in persuasion, or persuasive writing.

The goal of persuasion is to convince an individual or an entity regarding an idea, concept, opinion, or perspective. Persuasive writing is notoriously difficult; however, it is not impossible. This style of writing is a form of nonfiction that demands careful diction, the development of sound analytics throughout the writing piece, and a cohesive and integrated platform of ideas, arguments, and conclusions.

Effective persuasion requires a careful attention given to the audience and their needs. This must be done throughout the entire writing process of the editorial. Following a traditional writing formula will not be sufficient; rather, audience intent and interests, as well as their individual styles and ideologies must all be taken into consideration. This requires forethought and a keen understanding of the audience. This demands critical thinking.

Some key areas to keep in mind when writing persuasive pieces is to always respect your audience. Do not view your audience negatively, as this will come across in your actions and or your writing. It is important to consider the feelings and thoughts of your audience, and not take certain aspects of their patient, intelligence, or empathy for granted.

Remember that they are human too, and may feel just as strongly as you do regarding what you are trying to persuade them on. The mantra here is to know your audience. Make your writing readable or audience-focused, rather than your focus. Make sure that you focus on an argument that is best calculated to persuade your audience; your persuasive writing must be tailored to the needs and wants of your given audience.

Ignore your personal preferences; appeal to the preferences of your audience instead. You may have to think long and hard about what your audience wants, whether it is efficiency, cost-effectiveness, time needed for implementation, practicality, or feasibility. Make sure you know from what standpoint your audience is coming from, and then write from that perspective.

Always remember that your audience may not be persuaded immediately. Allow sufficient time for them to digest the information. If need be, continue to address your audience over time, and address specific needs or wants they bring up. Of course, you should not be pushy but rather be proactive. When considering your audience, you must understand that there are three likely scenarios possible:

o   You will change your audience's point of view.

- o You will bring your reader's point of view closer to your own. They may not be in total agreement with you, but they may have some respect and acceptance for your view.
- o You will fail to change your audience's mind, even having provided solid reasoning.

The outcome or your persuasive piece depends partly on how well you can understand and relate to your audience, and shape your information accordingly. You must make it convincing to them. Other aspects of your audience can impact your piece of their acceptance or rejection of it. The below are pointers for your consideration when writing a persuasive piece:

Experience: your audience may be experienced or novice readers. An individual who knows little about the given subject will need more background information than someone who is enlighten, or at least knowledgeable. The more experienced reader may need more detail, more evidence, and a more sophisticated level of analysis to be convinced.

The type of reader: your readers may be skeptical, neutral, or convinced. If your audience does not already agree with you, or is neutral, it will be much more difficult to persuade them. You have to work to establish common ground, acknowledge opposing views, and admit the strength of those opposing views where necessary and true. If your audience already agrees with you, it is obvious that you do not have to persuade them any further. Your goal in this case is to bring them to act or react in a certain way.

Type of appeal: emotional versus rational. Certain audiences respond more or less to emotion versus rationality. Some more skeptical or expert audiences may require more reason, such as examples, facts, and analyses.

They will respond more to factual arguments, and be less responsive to emotional appeal, and may view emotional appeal as manipulative. An audience who is familiar with a subject may respond well to emotional languages that act as a reinforcement to their points of views. Deciding how much emotion versus reason to put into your writing depends on a critical analysis of your audience.

Tips to Persuasive Writing

In persuasive writing, do not be negative. State your thesis in the first paragraph. Make your position clear. Your readers may not read the rest of your argument if you "turn them off" or make them mad. Avoid words like disgusting or awful. Using threatening words is absolutely not warranted in persuasion. This is never a good way to win over another person's opinion. Don't let your readers or audience make choice in extremities. When you make your readers choose between extremes, you are ignoring all the choices in-between.

Example: *"The president of the university says that students must get at least a "C" average if they are to play on school teams. If the rule goes through, we might as well stop playing right now".*

As a persuasive writer it is not good to toss in a Red Herring. That is to distract the reader from the real issues by tossing in another idea. The name comes from the old practice of drawing a dead fish across the trail of pursuing dogs to make them follow the wrong path.

Example: *"The Physical Instructor says that students must get at least a "C" average if they want to play on school teams. This is another example of how wrong-headed the Physical Instructor is. Doesn't he know that this is a democracy?"*

In persuasive writing, always avoid Bandwagon persuasion. To get on the bandwagon means to do what everyone else is doing. Writers who use this technique want you to think something is good just because everyone else is doing it.

Example: *"I can get a ride to the city center intellectual club for the class trip competition. We'll be gone for the entire weekend. Everyone is going, Dad/Mom!"*

It is important to always include your audience in your thinking. By using the editorial "we" it makes the reader feel like you are all on the same side of the issue. Furthermore, support your argument with facts and opinions. Base your facts on the most up to date information. You only need two or three well researched facts to support your argument. Most often opinions give person feelings or beliefs. The opinions of experts can be especially strong support for your strive to persuade people.

As a means of persuading your readers or audience, always look for a "hook" to grab your reader's interest. An incident or a powerful statistics is a good way to start a piece of persuasive writing. It is also good to think about your audience. That is, who will read your writing? Knowing who your readers are will help you decide what you need to tell them in your wiring.

Persuasive writing can be in the form of an essay, letter to the editor, a speech or a petition. The form of your writing and your audience will affect the content of your writing. In such cases, it will be of essence to give incidents and examples. These will help your readers relate in a personal way to your problem.

You must always be cognizant of the fact that people might oppose your position pen down. Try as possible to guess objections that people might have to your point of view. Then answer those objections. Be not perturbed by the objections and loose balance in your thoughts, organize your writing.

There is no right way to organize persuasive wiring. One way that often works well is start with your weakest argument and build to your strongest. You might also try by starting with ideas your audience will agree with and moving to those they might oppose. When you overcome this euphoric situation, your final paragraph should end with a powerful emotional appeal leaving your reader or audience feeling like they want to stand up and shout, "Yes, yes, we agree!"

The purpose of persuasion in Editorial Writing

In a persuasive editorial, you express an opinion about an issue of public interest. You support that opinion with facts, reasons, and examples, and communicate your viewpoint to a targeted audience or readers. A persuasive editorial should have the following characteristics:

- ✓ A topic that involves a matter of opinion
- ✓ An issue of public (rather than personal) interest
- ✓ A thesis statement that clearly expresses an opinion about that issue
- ✓ Specific facts, details, examples, and reasons that support the opinion
- ✓ Reasonable tone and persuasive language

A persuasive editorial presents an opinion about an issue of public interest. Opinions in this case deal with matters of interpretation, with questions that can be viewed in different ways. As stated earlier, when you plan to write a persuasive editorial, you need to know your audience. Ask the following questions to create an audience profile:

- o What issues are my readers or audience most concerned about?
- o Where do they live?
- o How much do they know about this issue? How are they likely to feel about it?
- o What is their comprehensive level?

Persuasive Techniques in Editorial Writing

The purpose of persuasion is to grab the attention of the reader, therefore for your editorial to be catchy, there are certain techniques you must employ in your introduction, comment and conclusion of your editorial piece. These techniques are stated below:

- Be mindful of your language. As you may be aware language is the key root of communication. Make sure your language must be void of ambiguity and must be meaningful
- The usage of simple words is the hallmark of communication. Always keep writing simple but maintain maturity and the stance of corporate venture. Your writing should not intimidate your reader with ballistic words that will not hammer in your message.

- First impression must be created. Your introduction paragraph must be sharp. It should not be scanty or sleepy. You must keep your readers in the mood of reading your piece.
- Always create the first impression just as meeting a friend for the very first time. This impression can only be created in the opening paragraph of your piece. It is your responsibility to sustain the interest of the reader with all of the facts you propounding.
- In your writing, do not beat around the bush or ramble. Be exact of what you say or writing. In geography, what do you know about meandering? To help you, meandering is those tributary of rivers that circulate around to connect the main river outlet. So in editorial writing, you don't have to meander. In your conclusion paragraph, it must be appealing for your reader to be persuaded.

Know Your Audience

It is important to know that you cannot persuade your listeners if you do not know much about them. Knowing your listeners helps you to shape your message in a way that will most likely gain their acceptance. What is more troubling is when your goal is to persuade, and you cannot simply inform, your audience the proper way. Persuasion and editorial are key to making your readers or audience convinced of what you are communicating to them.

For any content editorial piece you opt to release to the consumers, is important to know who is reading your editorial. Writing editorials without knowing the target group you are writing for is like jumping into the sea to swim when in fact you do not know how to swim. As an editorial writer, it is important to know your audience or target group(s) in order to exponentially increase the impact of your editorial. It is a cardinal effect if you are writing for a specific audiences so you know how to deal with the issues based on your varied audiences.

CHAPTER TEN

PROPAGANDA AND EDITORIAL WRITING

IT IS INDISPUTABLE THAT PROPAGANDA and media are inseparable. Mass media, as a system for transmitting and relaying information and messages to the public, play a role in amusing, entertaining and informing individuals with rules and values that situate them in social structure. In this regard, propaganda and the mass media, especially editorial analyzes an unspecified issues including domestic, regional, and global concerning Africa and world news coverage of events or happenings such as in West Africa.

If we can reflect on the popular insurrection in Burkina Faso, West Africa, the long -term leader Blaise Campaore was forced from office in 2014 following his almost 27 years role as president. It was through the media the International Crisis Group (ICG) was able to note that "the opposition is divided and lacks financial capacity and charismatic experience leaders and none of the key figures in the ruling party has emerged of a credible successor". This observation by the ICG was noticed from the massive reportage of the media of which editorial and propaganda cannot be void from.

Another case and point to attribute a glaring contribution of the media and propaganda through reports including editorial is the ongoing Casamance conflict in Senegal between the Government of Senegal and the Movement of Democratic of Democratic Forces of

Casamance (MFDC). Although the conflict is at low level but because of media reports it has claimed the attention of the international community. Presently, there is a deployment of international troops in Senegal striving to quell the crisis.

Going further on propaganda and editorial writing, it is important to reflect on the historicity of propaganda so as to give a clear intellectual understanding. Even though you are reading mass communication, I am sure you came across some history courses. On this note, it will be safe to state that throughout the course of human history, people have witnessed a number of events that have been a source of pain and shame for them across the globe including Africa.

Examples of such pain and shame in Africa can be exampled in occurrences such as the Nigerian Biafra war that began in 1967 through 1970 that was reported by the British Broadcasting Corporation (BBC) in 1968, the 1979 coup d'état of Ghana that was reported by the Voice of America (VOA) of the same year as well as the crises in Liberia that started in late 1989 through 2003 and was constantly reported by the international media, particularly the B. B. C. From 1989 up to the signing of the Accra Comprehensive Peace Accord (ACPA) at the "M" Plaza Hotel in Accra, Ghana in 2003.

Similar civil upheavals also occurred in Sierra Leone from 1991through 2002 and the Cote d'voire in the early 2000s as reported by the B. B. C. These civil wars and crises were exacerbated through propaganda by the media, especially radio reports. If we are to recount the entire global trend of events that brought pain and shame for people, particularly the war scenarios just mentioned above, you will agree that propaganda plaid a major role in these occurrences.

Bernays & Miller(2005) noted that the removal and relocation of the native people in North America, the Jewish Holocaust of the Second World War, and the ethnic cleansing of Tutsis in Rwanda during the early 1990s are occurrences that inflected mayhem on people through propaganda. Nevertheless, while each of these represents the worst aspects of humanity, they are also an example of the successful use of propaganda.

From the above mentioned, it can be inferred that propaganda is a mode of communication used to manipulate or influence the opinion of groups to support a particular cause or belief. Over the centuries, propaganda has taken the form of artwork, films, speeches and music among other forms of communication.

Propaganda is not exclusively negative, it often involves emphasis on the benefits and virtues of one idea or group, while simultaneously distorting the truth or suppressing the counter-argument. For example in historical context, the Nazi party rose to power by promoting the idea that it would lead Germany out of economic depression, which it claimed was, among other things, the result of Jewish people stealing jobs from hard-working Germans (Ensor, 2013).

What is Propaganda?

Propaganda according to Ensor (2013) is information that is not objective and is used purposely to influence people and foster an agenda. Ensor (2013) noted that propaganda most often present facts selectively to encourage a particular synthesis or belief, or using loaded language to produce an emotional posture rather than a rational response to the information that is presented. Most times, propaganda is associated with material prepared by governments, but political parties, activist and pro-democracy groups, and the media can also produce propaganda (Ensor, 2013).

Ensor(2013) further stated that in the twentieth century, the word propaganda was associated with a manipulative approach, but propaganda historically was a neutral descriptive term. A wide range of materials and media are used for conveying propaganda messages, which changed as new technologies were invented, including paintings, cartoons, posters, films, pamphlets and radio shows.

In a literary debate Bernays & Miller(2005) argued that propaganda is making puppets of us. We are moved by hidden strings which the propagandist utilizes to manipulates. Etymologically, Prankanis (2001) asserted that propaganda is a modern Latin word, the gerundive form of propagare: meaning to spread or to propagate -- thus propaganda means that which is to be propagated. Originally, this word derived from a new administrative body of the Catholic church created in1622, called the Congregatio de Propaganda Fide meaning Congregation for Propagating the Faith, or its activity aimed at propagating the Catholic faith in non-Catholic countries. For Cohen (1996) he claimed that from the 1790s, the term began to be used also to refer to propaganda in secular activities with a pejorative or negative connotation in the mid-19th century, when it was used in the political sphere. Making further disclosure, he recognized the fact that propaganda was an instrument used to lured people to accept political ideology realizing that the minds of the people can easily be manipulated as long as convincing propaganda messages are pronounced (Cohen, 1996).

The Origin of Propaganda

In his writing Akaboge (2005) explained that the primitive forms of propaganda have been a human activity as far back as reliable recorded evidence exists. The Behistun inscription detailing the rise of Darius to the Persian throne is viewed by most historians as an early example of propaganda. Another striking example of propaganda during Ancient History according to Akaboge (20057) is the last Roman civil wars (44-30 BC) during which Octavian and Mark Anthony blamed each other for obscure and degrading origins, cruelty, cowardice, oratorical and literary incompetence as well as drunkenness and other slanders.

Propaganda during the Reformation period according to Akaboge (2005) helped in the spread of the printing press throughout Europe, and particularly within Germany -- that caused new ideas, thoughts, and doctrine to be made available to the public in ways that had never been seen before the 16th century. During the era of the American Revolution, the American colonies had a flourishing network of newspapers and printers who specialized in the topic on behalf of the Patriots.

Akaboge (2005) recorded that the first large-scale and organized propaganda of government propaganda was occasioned by the outbreak of war in 1914. After the defeat of Germany in the First World War, military officials such as Erick Ludendorff suggested that British propaganda had been instrumental in their defeat. Adolf Hitler came to echo this view, believing that it had been a primary cause of the collapse of morale and the revolts in the German home front and Navy in 1918, there by expounding his theory of propaganda that provided a powerful base for his rise to power in 1933 (Akaboge, 1942).

Stressing further, Akabogel (2005) noted that in the early 20th century, the invention of motion picture gave propaganda a powerful tool for advancing political and military interests when it came to reaching a broad segment of the population and creating consent or encouraging rejection of the real or imagined enemy adding that the motion picture plaid a pivotal role in the disorganization of the enemies strong holds.

Public Perceptions About Propaganda

In the early 20th century Ensor (1948) stated that the term propaganda was used by the founders of the nascent public relations industry to refer to their people. This image, according to Ensor (1948) died out around the time of World War II, as the industry started to avoid the word, given the pejorative connotation it had acquired. Literally translated from the Latin gerundive as "things that must be disseminated", in some cultures the term is neutral or even positive, while in others the term has acquired a strong negative connotation (Ensor, 1948).

The connotations of the term propaganda according to (Ensor,1948) can also vary overtime. For example, in Portuguese and some Spanish language speaking countries, particularly in the Southern Cone, the word propaganda usually refers to the most common manipulative media, especially in advertising. Continuing his views Ensor (1948) noted that in English, propaganda was originally a neutral term for the dissemination of information in favor of any given cause. During the 20th century, however, the term acquired a thoroughly negative meaning in western countries, representing the international dissemination of often false, but certainly compelling claims to support or justify political actions or ideologies (Ensor, 1948).

According to Laswell (1928) the term began to fall out of favor due to growing public suspicion of propaganda in the wake of its use during World War I by the Creek Communities in the United States and the Ministry of Information in Great Britain. He furthered that in democratic countries, the official propaganda bureau was looked upon with genuine alarm for fear that it might be suborned to party and personal ends. For those of you students that monitor political activities and governmental operations in Africa, especially within the ECOWAS Sub-Region, you might have noticed that what is obtaining in the Western World by using their bureau or Information Ministries for propaganda purposes is replicated in Africa using the ministers of information to propagate the workings of the government even when such propagations are not in the interest of the citizens.

From experience, most university students do not have time to monitor radio or read newspapers rather they are glued to their "MP-4" or other musical gargets. From this reading, if you are one of those who don't monitor the news, please make it a duty to start monitoring radio or the local dailies, particularly you students of mass communication so as to get you informed on happenings around you and in the global community. This habit of monitoring the media will carry you a long way in your professional sojourn.

You should understand by now that the public's discovery of propaganda has led to a great of lamentation over it. Propaganda has become an epithet of contempt and hate, and the propagandists have sought protective coloration in such names as 'public relations officer,' 'specialist in public education' or 'public relations adviser'. Propaganda by my learning is a concerted set of messages aimed at influencing the opinions or behavior of large numbers of people. And one who disseminates propaganda is a propagandist.

Editorial is the means of expressing opinion to convincing or persuading people to effectuate to change or cause them to take action. In this connection, propaganda cannot be divorced from editorial writing, especially when the editorial is projecting an issue that would warrant action. However, there is dichotomy between propaganda and editorial in that, propaganda make things to appear what they are not really are and editorial is the advancement of opinion of any news entity concerning society and its people.

Types of Propaganda

Identifying propaganda has always been a problem. The main difficulties have involved differentiating propaganda from other types of persuasion, and avoiding a biased approach. Samuels (2011) defines propaganda as a systematic form of purposeful persuasion that attempts to influence the emotions, attitudes, opinions, and actions of specified target audiences for ideological, political or commercial purposes through the controlled transmission of one-sided messages which may or may not be factual via mass and direct media channels.

The definition focuses on the communicative process involved or more precisely, on the purpose of the process, and allow propaganda to be considered objectively and then interpreted as positive or negative behavior depending on the perspective of the audience or readers. Based on the above definition, it can be perceived that propaganda is a communication tool that is mainly used to influence an audience or group of people to foster an agenda or selectively presented facts to enhance a particular idea that would result to an emotional response.

According to the historian Zeman (1965) propaganda depicts the colors of white, grey or black. Giving a symbolic explanation of propaganda colors, Zeman (1965) noted that that white propaganda openly discloses its source and intent while the grey propaganda has an ambiguous or non-disclosed source or intent and the black propaganda purports to be published by the enemy or some organization besides its actual origins. These colors of propaganda Zeman (1965) noted can be compared to underground operation -- a type of clandestine operation in which the identity of the sponsoring government, entity or person is hidden. In scale, these different types of propaganda can also be defined by the potential of true and correct information to compete with the propaganda (Zeman, 1965).

Explaining on the colors of propaganda, Zeman (1965) stated that opposition to white propaganda is often readily found and may slightly discredit the propaganda source while opposition to grey propaganda, when revealed often orchestrated by an inside source, may create some level of public outcry. Opposition to black propaganda according Zeman (1965) is often unavailable and may be dangerous to reveal, because public cognizance of black propaganda tactics and sources would undermine or backfire the very campaign the black propagandist supported.

In such situation, the propagandist seeks to change the way people understand an issue or situation for the purpose of changing their actions and expectations in ways that are desirable to the interest group. Propaganda, in this sense, serves as a corollary to censorship in which the same purpose is achieved, not by filling people's minds with approved information, but by preventing people from being confronted with opposing points of view. What sets propaganda apart from other forms of advocacy is the willingness of the propagandist to change people's understanding through deception and confusion rather than persuasion and understanding.

The leaders of organizations know the information to be one -- sided or untrue, but this may not be true for the rank and file members who help to disseminate the propaganda. If you recap keenly on occurrences on the global community, especially in Africa you will get to know that there exist conspicuously five types of propaganda as listed below:

Wartime propaganda-This propaganda is a powerful weapon in war; it is used to dehumanize and create hatred toward a supposed enemy, either internal or external -- by creating a false image in the mind of soldiers and citizens. This can be done by using derogatory or racist terms. Let's look right to our doorsteps, West Africa, most of the wars are propagated by the media especially the Western media. Think about the incursion of the Liberian civil crisis on 24th December 1989, the civil upheaval of Gambia, Ivory Coast, and the civil unrest of Guinea, all these crises occurred in recent years where propaganda by the media plaid a major role.

Religious propaganda-This propaganda was often used to influence opinions and beliefs on religious issues, particularly during the split between the Roman Catholic Church and the Protestant Churches. I am sure you came across the leader of the protester Martian Luther while you were doing your introduction to mass communication course, especially students majoring in mass communication. As a tip off, Luther protested against denying the public to information by the Catholic Church. He led the advocacy for the public to be informed by circulating whatever information that had impact on their lives. More in line with the religious propaganda, this propaganda is also used widely in debates about new religious movements such as Bok haram of Nigeria, the Muslim Fundamentalists of Egypt, the recent pronouncement to build a good number of mosques in the Gambia, and the move by some Christians to Christianize Liberia.

Political propaganda–Political propaganda has become more common in political contexts, in particular to refer to certain efforts sponsored by governments, political parties, but also often with covert interests. If you carefully study the political culture and orientation of Africa, you will notice that propaganda also has much in common with public information campaigns by governments, which are intended to encourage or discourage certain forms of behavior. Again, the emphasis is more political in propaganda. Propaganda can take the form of leaflets, posters, newspapers, Television (TV) and radio broadcasts and can also extend to any other media outlets.

Advertisement propaganda - Journalistic theory generally holds the view that news items should be accurate, balance, credible, and objective, giving the reader an accurate background and analysis of the subject on hand. On the other hand, advertisements evolved from the traditional commercial advertisements to include also a new type in the form of paid articles or broadcasts disguised as news. These generally present an issue in a very subjective and often misleading manner, primarily meant to persuade rather than inform. Normally they use only subtle propaganda techniques and not the more obvious ones used in traditional commercial advertisements. If the reader believes that a paid advertisement is in fact a news item, the message the advertiser is trying to communicate will be more easily "believed" or "internalized". Such advertisements are considered obvious examples of "covert" propaganda because they take on the appearance of objective information rather than the appearance of propaganda, which is misleading.

The Importance of Propaganda in Editorial Writing

Most people consider propaganda as glaring lies or a diabolical communication strategy, but in essence, propaganda could be used in responsible and serious minded journalistic and communication messages like editorial writing. Nonetheless, propaganda is a rational use of argument and sound emotional appeals to convert or influence behavior either for positive or negative believes that propaganda could be useful for if the editorial writer apply the right techniques.

Propaganda Techniques in Writing Editorial

It is an undisputable fact that Propaganda techniques are useful raw materials in editorial writing. According to Okoro & Agbo(2003) propagandist techniques would enable the editorial writer to gain superior edge over competition and win support in the process of crusading for a cause or executing a campaign. Ate (2006) captured some propagandist techniques in the followings ways:

- ○ **Casting of blanket generalities** –This propaganda technique is usually used to make broad report about an entire group. To buttress the communication expert Ate, during the emergence of independence in Africa when education was in its embryonic stage introduced by missionaries, most Europeans perceived African students as not having interest in education because their African parents were not opting for western education. This was not the case. Bringing western education to Africa at the time was a strange phenomenon due to the cultural diversities. It called for cultural assimilation at the time, but not being interested in education as was perceived by the adventured Europeans.
- ○ **Name calling** – Name calling technique in propaganda could be used either negatively or positively. "Bad name is given to whatever the propagandist wants the public to reject or condemn without examining the evidence. For example, the

opponents may be labeled detractors, labor union executives as destabilizers" (Okoro and Agbo, 2003).

On the other hand with a positive and softer perspective, names like honey, sweetie, darling, my dear to mention a few carry strong torrents of love from the addresser to the addressee.

o **Card stacking** – In their aversion Okoro & Agbo (2003) noted that this device or technique is the act of presenting one side of the coin. The propagandist advertises or highlights some aspects in an issue he wants the public to know and covers up or down plays those he doesn't want the public to know. In this form of propaganda, strong and concrete facts, vivid illustration and profound statements are used in achieving the desired result.

o **Transfer aggression** – Here the propagandist encounters with a person or group of persons of a certain tribe and in dealing with the issue he cast the blame on the entire tribe. Say for instance, all of tribe 'A or B' are not good people.

It is important to note that every editorial that is worth of its substance must be spiced up with persuasive elements if it must win the affection of the audience or readers. It is therefore expedient for every editorial writer to understand the nitty-gritty of persuasion and utilize same for effective case making.

CHAPTER ELEVEN

STEPS AND TIPS IN EDITORIAL WRITING

Steps to Writing an Editorial

As STATED IN EARLIER READINGS, you will definitely agree that writing an editorial is a research based venture. The writer will have to find a subject that is of substance to write about. After that, the editorialist will have to do research so as to collect relevant information on the subject matter. Writing an editorial is a professional undertaken that calls for proactive planning and creativity.

As an editor or reporter (journalist), asked to write an editorial piece for your media institution, it will be a welcoming sign that your career is looking up. For any journalist or mass communicator to be asked to write an editorial is a matter of great privilege and honor. As opposed to regular news reports, an editorial is more about opinions than just the mere facts. It is meant to express a specific opinion about a current issue of news.

As an editorial writer, you should always consider the below steps:

- *Choose your topic wisely*
  For the editorial to have the required or maximum impact, choose an issue that has been making the headlines in the news

recently. For instance, if the presidential elections are around the corner, focus on a particular political topic. In this direction, be very specific about the issue you wish to focus on. There are enormous issues that may be featured in the edition of the newspaper, but should narrow down your area of interest with as much precision as possible. Above all, make sure that the topic is relevant and timely. The topic chosen might be local but the write-up should not be parochial, that is, it should not be narrowly scoped. (*Get out of the box*). Be familiar with socio-political and economic issues of the day from where editorial topics are drawn.

In most cases, editorial topics could be borne out of the desire to amaze or amuse. There is no gainsaying the fact of editorial writing is a serious-minded affair. However, there are some situations where an editorial topic could be given light treatment to entertain the audience while feeding them with concrete facts. This is done to ease their tension and dilute the stress that usually goes with analysis of burning issues.

- *Declare your agenda outright*
  An editorial without an unquestionable opinion is bound to fall flat on its face. Right at the very start of the editorial, define your agenda in clear terms. Make sure that you state your opinion or thesis coherently. Remember about research and refresh your memory and concentrate on thesis statement writing skills.

- *Build your argument*
  A good editorial expresses your point of view while a great one manages to persuade other to join the camp of thoughts. In order to persuade people, you need to have a sound argument based on facts and comparison, not vitriol and diatribe. Once you have stated your thesis, acknowledge contradictory opinions and explain why you disagree with them. Always feel free to use facts, statistics, quotations and theoretical explanations for criticizing your opponents' views. Rejecting their views

outright without any explanation screams of cowardice and unprofessional ethics. To build a foolproof argument, you will need to achieve a balance between content and style. Not only will you need substantial data, you will also need to structure it coherently.

- *Strengthen your argument with analogies*
  Nothing disarms your opponent better than cultural, social or political analogies. For instance, if you are writing about a controversial issue like secret surveillance on university campuses, look for similar instances in other countries and how they tackled those problems. You can use such an analogy to your benefit by highlighting both similarities and the differences. You can flag the issue at the Kwame Nkrumah University in Ghana and compare same at the University of Ibadan in Nigeria or the University of Sierra Leone. This will also be a good time to speak about the ultimate consequences of a policy if appropriate action is not taken by concerned agencies or stakeholders.

- *Provide possible solutions*
  Now, you have made a case for your views and demolished your opponents' claims. Mind, this is not the end of the editorial journey. An editorial is primarily meant to indulge in constructive criticism that is, even though it critiques one point of view, it must be able to provide possible alternative. Say for instance, your editorial attacked the efficacy of steps taken by the government to curb drug abuse in the country, conclude your piece by discussing other viable options.

Once again, build an argument and talk about why your proposed steps are better than the ones already advanced by the government. Don't mistake an editorial for an opportunity to indulge in mindless or vague criticism, be objective to offer a better vision for the future in the interest of the popular majority.

Structure of Editorial

Editorials are written according to well established formula just as in geometry or fraction. Editorials cannot just be written in a vacuum. There must be a probing issue of public concern and such issue must be directed to a specific target group or audience. A typical editorial has five parts. They include the title, introduction, body, solution and conclusion.

In any editorial writing exercise, you must have a title. The title defines or introduces the editorial. It should be active, interesting and less wordy. Since titles serve as windows to editorials, they should not be dull, ambiguous or misleading. Title must be catchy, sharp, and punchy or appealing.

The introduction or lead is simply the first paragraph of the editorial. Like the editorial title, the lead or introduction must be captivating and juicy in order to compel the reader to read the entire editorial piece. The opinion is expressed in the body. This contains the ingredient and substance of the editorial. It is the place where the pros and cons of an issue are analyzed; conflicts of different colors are raised and resolved in the body of an editorial. Solution in the editorial offers a solution to the problem and the conclusion emphasizes the main issue.

Additional Tips on Structuring the Editorial

In writing the editorial lead with an objective explanation of the issue or controversy, include the five W's and the one H. Also include facts and quotations from sources which are relevant to the editorial. Always present your opposition first. As the writer you disagree with the opponent's viewpoints. Identify the people (specifically who oppose you). *Use facts and quotations to state objectively their opinions.* Give a strong position of the opposition. Understand that you gain nothing in refuting a weak position.

To have an edge over the oppositions, refute their beliefs. In such a case, you can begin your article with transition. Pull in other facts and quotations from people who support your position. Always concede a valid point of the opposition which will make you appear rational, one who has considered all the options.

In defense of your position, give reasons from strong to the strongest order. Use a literary or cultural allusion that lends to your credibility and perceived intelligence. In the conclusion of the editorial you must conclude with some punches. Give solutions to the problem or challenge the reader to be informed.

A quotation can be effective, especially if from a respected source. A rhetorical question can be an effective concluder as well. A position is always taken to effectuate the needed impact on the readers or stakeholders. A good conclusion of an editorial should leave a mark of a food for thought for the consumers or audience. Conclusion must lay emphasis on issue of spectacular in the editorial piece.

Why is Focus Important in Editorial Writing?

You will agree that focus is a concentration of attention. Focus in any write-up is very pivotal. As focus is important in feature writing, so it is in editorialwriting because it will assist the writer in choosing a topic that is manageable or narrow enough to handle. Focus to some degree will assist the editorial writer in defending the boundary of what is useful to the target audience.

Focus in this aspect of editorial writing can only be achievable through discipline on the part of the editorial writer and through environmental screaming.

CHAPTER TWELVE

ETHICS AND EDITORIAL

LET US UNDERSTAND A SIMPLE premise in dealing with this chapter. Ethics deals with moral issues while editorial deals with the expression of opinion of the media organization. In this regard, ethics and editorial strive to promote the free exchange of editorial information that is accurate, balance, fair, and complete or thorough. As an editorial writer, you must demonstrate ethical integrity that would bestow trust and confidence on your media institution. When these four principles which serve as the foundation for ethical fulfilment, readers of your editorial article would be encouraged to respect your media entity.

Just in case you might not know, in the practice of mass communication or journalism of which editorial is a part, reputation is the news organization through its reporters is the legal reliance or license, and the public trust is the stamped credential or certification. A good media institution must opt its editorial writer to gain them, and keep them in the interest of the entity. This is why it is important for every media institution to have a code of ethics to help provide guidelines on how to follow the ethical code.

To the contrary, if your media institution through your editorial reports act unethically too often your institution loses value in the eyes of the public. Media ethics through editorial articles promote and positively defend values such as a overwhelming respect for life and the rule of law and legality. As an editorial writer, you must bear in mind and be cautious that ethics defines and deals with ethics questions about how editorials should use contents for the consumption by the citizens.

General Ethical Issues

Before an editorial writer starts to write an article, he or she will have to ponder as to how to deal with the issue. The professional writer may be casual, even slovenly, in dress, habits, and attitudes, but never in the approach to the article. There is much the writer must dig through before writing. The interview notes may be lost somewhere among the stack of tape recordings and transcriptions, the library clip files, the volumes of studies and statistics, receiving calls from the field warrants the writer to pause and ponder. What does it all mean, and how am I to deal with it? In most cases, the writer will realize that what he or she does is frighteningly important.

A beginning editorial writer usually is surprised and, ever so briefly, elated to learn that he or she suddenly is a person of influence, a purveyor of wisdom, a molder of opinion and a shaper of society. The first of trill may come when some respected person volunteers "I read the other day that editorial piece, and the information, offered with authority", turns out to be from the issue the reporter has written on. The first letdown comes when someone charges that newspapers print was nothing but lies or you get your first growing phone call that usually begins, "I just want to let you know what your editorial has done to my entity, and you are not going to get away with such obscenity."

The fact is, what you write inevitably touches other people's lives, and editorials published in newspapers really can ruin lives, just as they can make celebrities and causes of the obscure and dispossessed. Consequently, no other profession perhaps, is so obsessed with ethics, nor so roundly condemned for its transgression. The reason for this is obvious. Most people depend on journalist to tell them the truth. So when you sit down for the first time to write a publishable editorial, just remember that several millions of people are depending on you for positive analysis.

Fortunately, this is not a burden you will bear alone as the progenitor of the article. Editors considered as gatekeepers of information get paid to help save you from your ignorance and cockiness. The first thing editors must do is to correct those elements that could get them and their newspaper sued, for instance glaring errors of fact. However, editors do not get paid to do your job for you. For this reason, in larger newspapers, editors prefer to hire experienced reporters who are not prone to beginners' mistakes.

Advocacy Journalism

Always understand that you are a journalist and not a propagandist. Do not plan to come into the profession with causes to fight and crusades to wage war. Your duty, in fact, often will be to struggle through the propaganda, the growing publicity and special interest type in order to get at the honest issues and information. In Africa, few newspapers today practice in their pages or columns what is known as advocacy journalism, the concept of stacking the facts so as to prove one side of an issue or take a position of the newspaper.

The actual duty at most newspapers is left, to editorial writers and feature columnists. That does not mean that some desk editors will not suggest a particular slant on a story, expecting you to play up a certain angle he or she considers especially important. In such cases, the editor will usually expect you to exhibit some objectivity.

If you are overly obsessed with certain points of view, you probably will betrouble in this profession and maybe should consider writing political tracts or working for one of advocacy institutions. After some conditioning in the mass communication or journalism profession, you will find that few causes deserve reverence. Not even charities are without their villains. Like so many other things in the profession, for inclination to push someone's propaganda usually is healed with experience. Furthermore, editors simply will not let you get away with personal advocacy. They might request you to wear "stop the war" button, but they will not let you rail in the print against the people.

Moreover, editors will not let you read people's minds. If somebody didn't say it or you don't see it, chances are that your editors will not let you write it. Exploring a subject's thoughts and motives, writing without how something might have happened or didn't, are devices used to give the tone of novels. In short, if you don't know it, don't say it or write it. This book is not negating the fact that you cannot advocate in your editorial writing, but your advocacy must be in the interest of the popular majority not an individual or a segmented few to the detriment of society or your personal aggrandizement.

Briberies as a Menace

Bribery is not a strange word or phenomenon in Africa as manifested in persistent reports on rampant corruption in the various local dailies not only in African media but also in Western media. You probably will never be offered a direct bribe, but you may be surprised to find how many people wanting to buy you lunch, give you tickets to movies and football games among other offers. They may not even like you, but they may like what your access to the reading public can do for them.

Therefore, let me sound a caveat that some people will try to use you by giving you enticing gifts. As a professional mass communicator or journalist assigned to writing editorials, you must stay off receiving such gifts. The problem is to know when the gift is trivial exchange between friends, or even a simple courtesy, and when it is an attempt to court your favor. If your mind can be refreshed on the Watergate episode in the United States, after the Watergate episode of the early 1970s, bank accounts and business transactions seemed to have become the object of media security, newspaper publishers became increasingly cautious about the habit of their employees. As the late legendary musician Bob Manley puts it in one of his lyrics, "If you are living in a glass house do not throw stones."

Consequently, from this Watergate episode many newspapers in the Western bloc and trickled down to Africa, established written guidelines on ethics in an effort to spell out what a reporter can and cannot do regarding gifts and associations. Usually such guidelines include warnings against accepting free services that might tend to compromise the integrity of the media entity. Such guidelines, of course, are designed mainly to spare media organizations ethical embarrassments, but they also offer reasonable checkpoints for developing personal standards for operating within the profession.

As in all things or professions, the best policy is honesty, and there probably is no other profession where most people count on you to be honest than the press or media of which you are going to be a part. With the awesome power comes a reciprocal awesome trust. Only the sleaziest of media entities will encourage any action that leads to taint that trust.

Ethics in Editorial Writing

Let it be understood that writing editorial guidelines covering ethical issues is an ongoing process that needs to reflect what is acceptable and what is not acceptable in a changing environment depending on the actors in the society. In view of this, let me be clear by saying that this book might not give you all of the guidelines or code of conducts that could be used as guide in writing your editorial. However, an understanding must be vivid in order to have an appreciable knowledge involved in ethics of editorial writing.

On this premise, ethics can be perceived as a professional integrity which I strongly believe is the bedrock or cornerstone of the profession's credibility, be it a mass communicator or journalist. Regardless of what profession you are positioned in globally, it must exclusively falls within the realm of code of ethics centering on public trust, truthfulness, fairness, integrity, independence and accountability. Virtually every profession in the world is guided by certain codes of conduct. Mass communication or journalism as profession is also governed by certain norms, creeds or cannons.

Reflecting on the African perspective, you will agree that we are governed by cultural norms that warrant respectability for the elders and those in authority, these norms are not just to be over looked because of Western cultural infusion. If you were in the remotest part of an African village, especially West Africa and you have a burning issue with an elder in that village, you dear not confront or challenge the elder in the village, if you did, you will be dealt with according to laid down policy protecting the cultural values of the village. Why do it in the city where some journalists lambast heads of states (presidents) and other government officials under the canopy of free speech and democracy?

In light of this, you cannot be a journalist or editorial writer in the city and you overlook the norms governing the professional ethics for your survivability. Ethics according to Harmon (1998) is a system of behavior, expectations and morals comprising standards of conduct for a population or profession. In essence, Harmon (1998) is portraying that ethics are general science of right and wrong. In its simplistic form Ethics are code of conduct which defines standards of behavior and morality for members of society or a given profession. Duyile (2005) describes media ethics as the "Moses of journalism" and insisted that the journalist, who wants to remain in the profession for life time career, will do himself or herself a lot of good if they avail themselves with the ethics of this noble profession.

In his view, Dickey (1979)agreed that the word ethics originated from the Greek word ethikos (moral) and ethos (character) which refers to the values or rules of conduct held by a group of individuals. In concurrence to Dickey (1979), it will be undisputable to say that in editorial writing, certain qualities are expected of editors, writers, and other media practitioners to adhere to the ethics in order to maintain high journalistic fray. Ethics are necessary to ensure sanctity and inculcate discipline within any given profession. I need not waste your time on which institution should ensure and enforce the ethical function of the media in your country.

Notwithstanding, as student of mass communication or journalism who are not practicing the profession, let me provide you a leeway to institutions responsible for the enforcement of ethical issues regarding the media. If you are a student in Nigeria, contact the Nigeria Press Council (NPC). If you are in Liberia, contact the Press Union of Liberia (PUL), in Sierra Leone; contact the Press Union of Sierra Leone (PUSL) or wherever you find yourself in the continent go to the media umbrella institution for further inquiry. You will get to know how they handle ethical issues in those various media institutions.

Every media institution must be guided by the following ethics or code of conduct though there is room for more ethical issues:

- **Editorial integrity and independence** – A news entity must have editorial integrity and independence in order to fully serve its readers or audience. Those who place hope in the news institution need to be confident that editorial decisions are neither influenced by political or commercial pressure nor by any personal interest. Issues relating to the content of the news should be the responsibility of professional journalists.

- **Fairness and Accuracy** – A media institution producing inaccurate or false information will ruin its credibility and those of the journalists attached to the media entity. Accuracy is always more important than speed. Do not be a herd's journalist or your institution. It is best to be second and get it right rather than first and get it wrong. The audience has the right to know that factual, accurate, balanced and fair reporting is the ultimate objective of good journalism and basis of earning public trust and confidence. It will not do you good to publish inaccurate and misleading information. It will kill your institution and it will render you or the institution great financial challenges.

- **Balance and Impartiality** – If your media entity is to win the trust and confidence of the public, particularly readers or audiences, impartiality must be the basic foundation of the media institution. To achieve this goal, the content must reflect all relevant sides in the stories where possible. Furthermore, provide room for the reader or audience to draw its own conclusion based on facts and make a clear distinction between factual information and opinion.

- **Decency** – Dress code in the profession is a paramount. A journalist should dress and comport him or herself in a manner that conforms to public taste. *Reward and Gratuity* – A journalist, especially an editorial writer should neither solicit nor accept bribe, gratuity or gratification or patronage to suppress or publish information. It is the right of the public to know. *Respect the privacy of others* -As a general rule, journalists should respect the privacy of individuals and their families, except in the case it affects public interest.

In concluding on this note, ethics in editorial writing is revolved around integrity, decency and honesty, in the course of discharging your fundamental social responsibility. As repeatedly stated, journalist are not expected to be induced in the course of their journalistic duties. Always uphold the tenets of the profession. Except otherwise, do not disclose your source of information to anybody. Understand that confidentiality is the hallmark of the profession.

CHAPTER THIRTEEN

THE ROLE OF EDITORIAL IN NATIONAL DEVELOPMENT

IN DEALING WITH THIS CHAPTER, it is important to understand the role of the media and what is development in the context of nation building. In this regard, the media with specificity to editorial is important in shaping the developmental agenda of any country. This is achieved through its constructive role in society by increasing public awareness of collecting views, information, and the attitude of the people towards certain issues. On the other hand, development is the process that fosters growth, progress, positive change or the enhancement of physical, economic, environment, and social activities aimed at improving the lives of the people and nation.

Putting it context, it can be implied that editorial is used as a multidimensional vehicle utilized for action, organization and communication that promotes economic, social and cultural factors. Development involve changes or advancement in nation building aimed at improving the political, economic and social lives of the people. With this understanding, it can be construed that the media through editorials play a vital role in the development of any nation, since they provide their traditional role of information, education, and entertainment, as well as additionally providing interpretation and social interaction in any society thereby helping with the development of the nation.

The Impact of Editorial on Political Actors

Putting the media in perspective, it is considered as autonomous actors in any political process. In editorials, media legitimately try to influence the agendas and decisions of the political system not only by explicitly expressing their opinions on issues and political actors, but also by assigning relevance to certain issues or sub issues and framing as well as interpreting political events according to their editorial stance. Globally, particularly in Africa it may be assumed that the impact of editorials on the political system depends on the degree of issue focusing and opinion consonance. If different newspapers consistently comment on the same issues and express similar opinions, considerable pressure is put on the political system.

Trager(2006) notes that to the growing demand for more transparency in politics and the pressure on political actors to legitimize their decisions it has become increasingly important for political actors to generate publicity and a favorable public opinion for their concerns. Yet, the term "public opinion" is still contradictory and poorly defined. Instead of following the common assumption that public opinion is the aggregate of individual attitudes, we proceed from the theoretically more substantial concept of public opinion as output of public communication.

Since the role of non-mediated public communication has continuously declined in modern societies, the media constitute the most important subsystem of the public sphere. According to Trager (2006) public communication is the open exchange of issues and opinions noticeable by a large audience, and is organized and structured by the media according to professional criteria and norms. Based on Trager's (2006) view, public opinion thus becomes visible through the contributions of various actors who advance their views on certain issues in both print and electronic media. These contributions may cover a variety of issues or concentrate on a few; they may represent consonant or dissonant opinions. Public opinion becomes a consistent and politically effective factor as a certain degree of correspondence develops regarding issues as well as opinions (Trager, 2006).

The crucial role of the media, particularly editorial in political communication is not restricted to mediating information between the political system and the audience. They do not only serve as neutral transmitters of information but also interpret and assess the events, issues and opinions they disseminate. They play an active role in the communication process by expressing their own views and opinions and trying to influence the agendas and attitudes of citizens and political actors.

Opinion in the media has often been subject to criticism. It is seen as a problematic bias rather than as a legitimate expression of the media's own views. Not the expression of opinion itself but the confounding of opinion and news is problematic. As long as opinion is marked as such the media have the right to take their own view and openly try to influence public opinion formation or even policy decisions.

If you will agree, it is noticed that in modern Africa, deliberation does not take place "face to face" any more, but is mediated by the mass media except in some isolated cases like seminars, conferences, or debates. Professional communicators, including political experts and journalists rather than ordinary citizens talk to each other and to the public. They assemble, explain, debate, and disseminate the best available information and ideas about public policy, in ways that are accessible to large audiences of ordinary citizens. The citizens form their opinions about relevant issues, adequate interpretations and possible solutions by paying attention to the information supplied by the media and by observing the discourse between the professional communicators (Gilbert, 2011).

The political actors themselves also need the media to observe public affairs. Thus, they do not only directly - in terms of "face to face" interaction - participate in the political process, but also collect information on issues and opinions through the media. The dissemination of information through the mass media is an undisputed media function in modern societies. It assigns media a predominantly passive role in the political process, providing a forum for a variety of political actors to express their particular views but not contributing their own view (Adams, 1997).

In Africa, Adams(1997) notes that media are also expected to supervise and criticize the political process, which puts them in a slightly more active position. Notwithstanding, this supervisory function has not led to a clarification of the degree of media activity, respectively the role of explicit or implicit opinion in media coverage. There are two main paradigms in my view which is opened to challenge. The media are either regarded as ordinary mediating agencies for events and issues without any consideration of political bias in selection and interpretation, or they are considered as manipulative and manipulated agencies influencing public attitudes and policy decisions without democratic legitimation.

Restricting the role of the media to an exclusive information agency, however, is not only a deficient description of the media but also means of distorting and underestimating the legitimate active role of the media in the process of opinion formation. In political communication processes the mass media are participating actors with genuine political interests and goals (Bowles & Borden, 2000).

Confounding the two aspects of media messages - the neutral dissemination and the media's autonomous contribution - leads to the perception of media as an uncomfortably diffuse factor in political communication. The claim of neutral information dissemination and the media's right to contribute to the political discourse as autonomous actors with their own voice thus have to be treated separately. Through editorials the media are explicitly authorized to publicly express their opinions and by noticeably commenting on public affairs they make use of their right to present themselves as autonomous actors.

Fox(2001) stresses that as a global phenomenon, editorials do not represent individual views of single journalists, but indicate the editorial stance of a media outlet as earlier stated in this book. It is assumed that media regard their editorials as a means to position and stabilize themselves on the audience market since editorial stance corresponds with certain political segmentations of the public. There are more liberal and more conservative media outlets and their distance to political parties differ considerably.

It is believed that editorials reflect the political view of the papers and serve as a forum of presentation for the media's own view of public affairs. Regarding the effects of media opinion in political communication, we need to distinguish between micro- and macro level effect. Whereas effects on the micro level refer to the impact of single editorials on individual recipients, macro level effects regard the impact of collective media opinion on public opinion formation and political processes.

Taking a macro level perspective we are not interested in single narrowly scoped editorials but in the universe of issues and opinions expressed in the media system especially when Africa is struggling for economic and democratic emancipation. Correspondingly, regarding media effects, the focus is not on individual opinion or behavioral change, but on the collective reaction to media opinion. It must be known how the political system reacts to collective media opinion.

The Role of Editorial in National Development

Sears(1985)notes that national development in this context is the ability of a sovereign nation or nations of any continent to improve the social welfare of its or their citizens by providing social amenities like quality education, potable water, agriculture, transportation, security, infrastructure, as well as medical care. In his expose' on the importance of the media, particularly editorials, development involves the creation of opportunities for the realization of human potentialities. Where the media comes in development process is through what is called "development communication". This is the type of communication which is consciously packaged by the sender such that the message content or the information sent could persuade, encourage or convince the receiver or target audience to adopt an attitude and participate in actualizing a development plan or goal.

At certain instances, the message sent aims at making the target audience adopt a positive attitudinal change towards a development purpose. To achieve this developmental goal, Miller(2013)advanced some indicators commonly used as measurement for national growth and development particularly in Africa. According to Miller (2013) the below listed are some of the indicators for national growth and development:

Gross Domestic Product (GDP)
Gross National Product (GNP)
GNP per capita

Birth and death rates
The Human Development Index (HDI)
Infant mortality rate
Literacy rate
Life expectancy

If the above indicators are to be manifested in the interest of the people, the role of editorial becomes very cardinal in creating the advocacy role to make sure that stakeholders, including political actors and state actors are intrigued in order to attain the desired developmental objectives for the people.

Relative to the above premise, Thomas Jefferson, an American founding father, principal author of the United States Declaration of Independence and the third United States president once said: "Were it left to me to decide whether we should have a government without newspapers, or newspapers without a government, I should not hesitate a moment to prefer the latter" (Malone, 1990).

The assertion of the former American president was stemmed from the fact that he had explicit confidence in the functionality of the press, especially newspapers at the time when views were expressed for the advancement of the American society. The president underscored the importance of the media inshaping the positive destiny of society particularly from editorial articles. In pursuit of accuracy, fairness and balance reporting, journalists will go to great lengths to talk to people in authority on issues of public interests.

For this reason, it is hoped that they are understood and officials, particularly national actors, will recognize the work journalists do. Quality journalism will happen if journalists are given the opportunity to access information that is important for the public good of society lifted in editorial pages. I am optimistic that as African students mastering mass communication or journalism, you are aware of the "Freedom of Information Act" rectified by most African presidents.

This Act gives you the opportunity and privilege to assess information from public officials in the interest of the society. It is my belief that the media is perceived as a collective means of communication by which general public or populace is kept informed about the day to day happenings in society through news reports, particularly editorial writings. As stated in earlier readings, the media is also said to be an aggregation of all communication channels that are used through techniques to make a lot of direct personal communication between the communicator and the public.

While talking of mass media however, the word "mass "means a large number of people or a collection and "media" means organs or channels of which editorial is a part. Hence mass media is a collection of organs of communication and information dissemination channels that reach out to a large number of people most often referred to as audience, receivers, readers or consumers. The information circulation is not only confined within members of the public, but it also serves to coordinate the information flow between government and the public and vice versa, in our own case, between leaders and the led and vice versa. In this process the editorial plays an important role in analyzing the happenings of society to effect any action that would contribute to its transformation.

The two broad categories of media including the Print media comprising of Newspapers, Magazines, Journals and Periodicals while the Electronic media which include Radio, Television and all related modern communication outlets such as Internet and social media are all compartments of editorials. Basically, the media are viewed as performing three functions or roles of information, education and entertainment.

These are the conventional social functions the media render to the public, but which is equally applicable in broader sense in national developmental pursuit. It is implicit that through educating, informing, and entertaining, the media is capable of building or making society. Therefore, society members of a nation particularly the leaders, should be aware of the importance of the media and foster actions aimed at enhancing national development.

Also added to these three basic roles of media is another role of persuasion, where media are seen as virile tools of applying persuasive methods to influence people's actions towards a particular direction. The mass media are therefore seen for their role in furnishing the public with necessary information to achieve development or change goals. These roles of the media in national development lie in their capacity and capability to teach, manipulate, sensitize and mobilize people through information dissemination.

As for Miller (2015) the media are also chart a course for the public in line with the agenda setting focus of stakeholders and the citizens, thereby creating in the minds of the people, issues that should be viewed as priority issues including development programs and policies. Instances of this role being presently played by the media in most African countries is the general millennium goal pursuit towards the year 2015, as proposed by the United Nations and incorporated as national policy by governments of member countries around the world.

Policies of the millennium goal touch on different aspects of health, education, children and women. The program could also be said to be part of the globalization pursuit to which any nation left out in its pursuance and implementation stands the possibility of being alienated in the comity of nations. In this regard, every nation, particularly Africa is striving to meet up with the millennium goal.

Though not free of some propagandist motives, health issues such as the HIV/AIDS, Polio Immunization and The Bird Flu Virus issues became the leading stories disseminated by the African media. Other related issues include wars, famine, women and children health and rights as well as democratization activities receive prominence and greater attention from the media. Another instance of developmental role by African media especially in West Africa, was the outbreak of the deadly Ebola virus. This virus exposed the weak health condition of three neighboring countries within the Mano River Basin and claimed the lives of thousands of their citizens.

Other Roles of Editorial (Media) in National Development

The media, particularly editorial in its totality is something that is very helpful in the developmental agenda of any country. There are a lot of positive aspects that help with the relationship between the media and national development. Having a vibrant media through its editorial columns can help to keep the society under control, which then helps contribute to the national development strive.

Development in a country is something that is very important and is a goal in many places. There are many different aspects reported in the media through editorial that are of the same functions globally including Africa. These aspects include demographic, economic, resource, politics, education, violence, health, and culture. There are also two goals that are set which help in developing a nation. These goals are economic and social.

Through its positive reportage in editorial write - ups, the media can create an enlightened society. This is a crucial prerequisite to nation-building because the more a people are informed the more they become enlightened and the more they would refrain from doing practices that will be inimical to the process of nation-building efforts. For example, citizens who will comprehend the message from editorials will always tend to be responsive to the ideals of nation-building.

By this, the citizens will not only obey state laws and preserve properties, but they will also participate in the drive of national development. Without this, no nation-building efforts will be set in earnest. National development requires a democratic society that allows the contribution of all, either rich or poor. With a responsible media, there will always be increase awareness in democratic participation.

This participation will in turn enhance national development initiative because the participation of all the citizens is counted in the drive for national building efforts. Also the media is very crucial in the formation of cross-cutting cleavages that embrace diversity. Accepting differences therefore are very important to national development because until we accept our differences and come together to build the nation, progress will be elusive. With a progressive media, this fear is allayed.

When properly utilized, media especially editorial correlates with national development. Both of them complement each other. A nation cannot be built without enlighten through the media. With media, citizens are nurtured that will enhance national development. In the same way, the media leads to efficient usage of a nation's resources because it serves as a watch dog on the different functionaries of society.

This stance of the media is very crucial to national development because without efficient usage of a nation's resources, nation-building will not be successful. This is evident in developed nations. To continue to build their nations, they do not only educate their citizens, but they greatly rely on the media because media shapes the attitudes, behaviors, and values of citizens. These are qualities that are needed for national development.

The media, especially editorial leads to formation of attitude through establishing of values for the society or nation and thereby building a climate of change in the society or nation. This involves the dissemination of news and information in response to the basic human need. Protection of Social Justice is another role of media in national development, in that the media are not only expected to record, compose or report account of events and stories just as the historians do, but the media are also expected to analyze issues through editorials and facts contained in the news, in line with the need and interest of Social Justice.

Arnold (2003) pointed out that the media especially editorial is subordinate to a far higher goal in ensuring that public and private conduct are directed towards the greatest possible measure of justice in society. In order to ensure a peaceful national coexistence and progress, the media have before them the task of discouraging such negative issues as ethnicity, dictatorship in leadership like the military rule and of course discourage embezzlement of public funds, as it is the disturbing trend presently indulged by most politicians occupying positions of responsibilities and related public officers in the continent of Africa where is most of the time an outcry of persistence corruption as constantly reported by the Western media.

The responsibility of informing people about development projects and programs is another major role of media to national development. Such programs designed and proposed by policy makers could be entirely new to the people at whom they need to be enlightened, educated and mobilized by the media. Instances of such programs are the Universal Basic Education (U.B.E.), the Girl-Child Education, Adult Education, Fighting Drug Addiction and Trafficking. For instance, a continental campaign towards boosting agriculture and food production in Africa (Miller, 2015).

Offering solutions to problems is another developmental role of the media through their editorial columns. This is because they are not only expected to criticize government officials and condemn their actions, but to also serve as watchdog of the society. Furthermore, they should review, analyze, appraise or criticize, as the case may be, activities of the various governments within the African continent for example, to push for one currency operation on a regional bases, and the effectuating of a common border trade among African States.

It should be understood that the relevance of the media in almost all spheres of human existence cannot be overemphasized, especially in the area of national development. Also the exigent need for good governance, responsible and accountable leadership goes hand in hand with the need for active role of strong and equally disciplined media towards enlightening, mobilizing and sensitizing both the public and the stakeholders in this direction. It should also be a cognizant factor that the impossibility of having totally unbiased media, because even in the developed countries, media are most of the time engaged in conducting opinion polls or making comments that favored certain political parties or candidates.

However, the conscience of the media through editorial itself needs reorientation to shed off characteristics of the ravaging societal malaise which in some ways, affect the media themselves. In this connection, Miller(2015) pointed out that the role of information in the context of national development is no longer a matter of dispute, but rather, useful if only it is properly disseminated. In a pluralistic and diverse society such as Africa, we need an information order built on cordial relationship between the state and the media, between leadership and the citizens, between the elite and the people at the grassroots level.

In all this, the media have an important role to play, always taking into consideration the socio - cultural conditions under which they operate, but without losing sight of the universal commitments of the professional ethics. It is therefore incumbent upon you as mass communication students haven gone through the functionalities of feature and editorial writing operate within the peril of the profession whenever you are called upon to serve in the capacity of a mass communicator or journalist in any part of the world of course, keeping in mind the theories of communication.

FIND IN SUBSEQUENT PAGES PUBLISHED FEATURE STORIES AND EDITORIAL ARTICLES IN SOME REPUTABLE PUBLICATIONS WITHIN THE SUB –REGION AS APPENDIXES. IT IS YOUR PRIVILEGE TO READ AND ANALYSE THEM.

REFERENCES

Aamidor, Abraham. (1999). *Real Feature Writing.* Hillsdale, NJ: Lawrence Erlbaum Associates,

Adam, G. Stuart and Roy Peter Clark. (2005). *Journalism: The Democratic Craft.* New York: Oxford University Press.

Adams, Paul. (1997). *Writing Right for Today's Media.* Chicago: Nelson-Hall.

Ainsworth, David (2005). Studies in English Literature. Oxford, England. Oxford University Press

Akaboge, C.E. (2005). The ethical journalist and brown envelope syndrome University of Nigeria, Nsukka

Arnold, George T. (2003). *Media Writer's Handbook.* Boston: McGraw-Hill.

Ate, A. A. (2006). Editorial Writing. "Unpublished Work"

Awoyinfa, M. (1999). The Art of Feature Writing for Newspaper and Magazine. Ibadan Shaneson C. T.

Bernays, E & Miller, M. (2005). The Art of Propaganda. Brookly, NY.: Ig Publications

Berner, R. Thomas. (1999). *The Literature of Journalism*. State College, PA: Strata Publishing.

Bernstein, Theodore M. (1995). The Careful Writer: A Modern Guide to English. New York: Free Press.

Bowles, Dorothy A. & Diane L. Borden (2000). Creative editing. 3rd ed. Belmont, CA: Wardsworth.

Bloom, Stephen G.(2000). *Inside the Writer's Mind*. Ames: Iowa State Press.

Brande, Dorothea (1981). Becoming a Writer. Los Angeles: J.P. Tarcher, Boston

Cohen, Bernhard L, (19963). The Press and Foreign Policy. Princeton: Princeton University Press.

Daramola, I. (2003). Introduction to Mass Communication. 2nd ed. Lagos: Rothan Press

Dickey, B. (1979). History of Business Ethics. University of Chicago Press.

Duyile, D. (2005). Writing for the Media. A manual for African Journalists. Lagos Group Communication

Ensor, Jason D. (2013). Propaganda at Home. Holder and Stoughton. NY.

Fedler, Fred. (2000). *Reporting for the Print Media*. 7th ed. New York: Oxford University Press, 2000.

Fox, Walter. (2001). *Writing the News: A Guide for Print Journalists*. 3rd ed. Ames: Iowa State University Press.

Friedlander, Edward Jay and John Lee. (2003). *Feature writing for the print media* Boston: Allyn and Bacon, 2003.

Fry, Don. (1996). Writing Your Way: Creating a Writing Process. Writer's Digest Books. NY.

Garrison, Bruce. (2004)*Professional Feature Writing.* 4th ed. Mahwah, NJ: Lawrence Erlbaum.

Gilbert, Erik T. (2011): Africa in World History,3rd. Edition Pearson Publishing Company, London, England

Gilbert, Steve. (2011) The History of Development: From Western Origins to Global Faith, 3rd ed. Zed Books, Rockville.

Goring, Hermann. (1947). Ministry of Propaganda and Public Enlightenment. W. W. Norton & Company. NY.

Harmon, Willis. (1998). Global Mind Change: The Promise of the 21st Century. San Francisco, California. Bennett& Koehler Publishers

Harrower, Tim. (2007). *Inside Reporting.* Boston: McGraw-Hill.

Hennessy, Brendan. (2006). *Writing Feature Articles.* Burlington, MA: Focal Press.

Hutchison, Earl R. (2007). *The Art of Feature Writing.* New York: Oxford University Press.

LaRocque, Paula. (2003). The Book on Writing: the Ultimate Guide to Writing Oak Park, IL: Marion Street Press, 2003.

Laswell, Harold D. (128). Propaganda Techniques in the World War. Menosha, George Banta Publishing Company

Lewis, Jon E. (2003)*The Mammoth Book of Journalism.* New York: Carroll & Graf.

Lundahl, Mats. (2001): *From Crisis to Growth in Africa* Routledge, South Africa.

Malone, Dumas. (1990). *Jefferson and His Time: The stage of Monticello (Vol.6)* Little, Brown and Company, Boston, USA

McKinney, P. (1986). Basic Legal Research for Criminal Justice and the Social Sciences. West Publishing Company. Kingston, Jamaica

McKane, Anna. (2006). *News Writing.* Thousand Oaks, CA: SAGE Publications.

Mencher, Melvin.(1998). *Basic Media Writing.* 6th ed. New York: McGraw Hill.

Miller, E. A. (2015). The Role of the Media in Agenda Setting. Global Media Studies Productions, University of Michigan

Miller, Roger L. (2013): Economics Today: The Micro View, 17th Edition Pearson Publication Company, London, England

Mills, Eleanor et. All (2005). Journalists. 100 years of the best Writing and Reporting. New York: Caroll and Craft

Murray, Donald M. (2003)*The Craft of Revision.* 5th ed. Boston: Thomson/Heinle.

Okoro, N. & B. Agbo (2003). Writing for the Media Society. Nuskka: Prize Publishers

Perkins, David. (2003). Designing Games for Ethics: Models and Techniques. Hillsdale. NJ: Lawrence Eribaum Associates, Perseus Publishing.

Prantkanis, Anthony. (2001): *Age of Propaganda: The Everyday Use and Abuse of Persuasion.* H. Freeman and Company Limited.

Samuels, C. (2011). Propaganda in Perspectives. Theson, AZ Brown
    Bear Books

Sears, V. (1985). Morals and the Media: Ethics in Canadian Journalism.
    2nd ed. UBC Press

Trager, R. (2006). Journalism and Mass Communication. CQ Press;
    4th ed.

Ukonu, M. (2005). Fundamentals of Editorial Writing: Nsukka: Multi
    Educational and Services Trust.

Zeman, Z. A. B. (1963). Global Communications, International Affairs
    and the Media. Oxford Claremore's. UK.

APPENDIX 1

Some Feature Articles to Provide Further Guidance
Do Your Own Critical Judgment and Analysis

Note that with the exception of appendix 1, the other articles in appendixes 2 – 5 were published in reputable media outlets including an Anthology of Students' Articles Journal, University of Liberia, 2012/2013, and newspapers from Ghana and Liberia

Article1:unpublished

Written by: Richmond S. Anderson, Sr.

Title: "The Mounting Challenges of the LNTG Twist Liberians Hope"

With all the insurmountable problems experienced in its first year of administration, the National Transitional Government of Liberia (LNTG) remains determined to create a better future for the country.

After fourteen years of a devastating civil upheaval in Liberia, major former warring fighters finally converged at the famous "M Plaza Hotel" in Accra, Ghana to seek a common ground aimed at attaining lasting peace for their country Liberia. This convergence yielded fruition through the signing of the "Accra Comprehensive Peace Agreement" (A.C.P.A.) on 18ᵗʰ August, 2003, barely a week following the departure of former President Charles Ghangay Taylor from Liberia to Calabar in Nigeria after his compulsory resignation as president demanded by the Economic of West African States (ECOWAS) Authority.

The A. C. P. A. was signed by considered major former warring factions including the Liberians United for Reconstruction and Democracy (LURD), the Movement for Democracy in Liberia (MODEL) and the relegated Government of Liberia (GOL) according to Article XXI.4, "The authority of the NTGL shall be established and recognized throughout the territory of the Republic of Liberia, immediately upon its installation in Monrovia. Also, "The NTGL shall have control over the entire territory of Liberia". From all indications, this provision in the peace agreement clearly implied that a government of inclusion, cohesiveness, and oneness of purpose was hopefully expected by war - warried Liberians.

Disappointingly, it was to the contrary as most of the appointees in the NTGL government from the former warring factions were paying loyalty to their respective factional institutions instead of the Transitional government of inclusion. This situation seemed to have stagnated the effective functioning of the government headed by the Chairman of the NTGL C. Gyude Bryant.

This situation manifested itself in the disillusionment of most Liberians against the government, with utterances such as "the government is insensitive to the plight of the common people". A Liberian business tycoon who was out of business for nearly 15 years due to the civil conflict lamented, "conditions continue to degenerate in the country, it was our thinking that the coming of the NTGL would have improved our lives shattered all these years. I am not sure of going back in business with the present precarious condition in the country."

In his inaugural address on 14 October 2003, Chairman Bryant addressing the nation pledged his government's commitment to improving the livelihood of every Liberian by reducing the price of basic commodities such as rice, fuel, gasoline and kerosene among others. In accordance with this pronouncement, Chairman Bryant, addressing the nation in late November 2003, reduced the prices of basic commodities mentioned above to relatively affordable prices.

But barely two months following the reduction, had prices escalated which resulted to unbearable hardship for the less fortunate in society.

"Cries and disgruntlement everywhere, the people were indeed not satisfied. The civil servants have demanded their over 24 months of back pay incurred under the Charles Taylor administration. "Our children cannot go to school because of no money to register them," a university professor averred.

October 14, 2004 was exactly one year since the N. T.G. of Liberia came into existence following years of devastation and mayhem caused by the defunct warring factions including the National Patriotic Front of Liberia (NPFL), the former factions opposed to Charles Taylor the Independent National Patriotic Front Of Liberia (INPFL) headed by the then General Prince Y. Johnson, and other factions that enjoyed the country's wealth to the detriment of the Liberian people. Chairman Bryant definitely braved the storm in the midst of claims and counter claims from the still structured former warring factions. "We will not accept your appointments, you must have consultation with the parties to the peace agreement, as chairman you have no right to make decision without our input" are some of the utterances of former faction leaders who were assimilated in the government of inclusion. This was a great challenge for Chairman Bryant.

With his resolute will to accomplish the mandate of the Transitional Government, Chairman Bryant continued to outline the achievements of the government. "Upon taken office, we prioritized a new beginning of cordiality and sincerity about peaceful co-existence with countries near this capital. I personally visited the sisterly Republics of Guinea, Sierra Leone and La Cote d'Ivoire where we took the message of peace in an attempt to improve Liberia's strained relations with these neighboring countries." Chairman Bryant maintained. In line with his policy, Chairman Bryant during the year paid visits beyond the African continent, with many efforts made to foster a good relationship with the international community, after Liberia had had a bleak relationship with the world for 14 years as a result of the civil conflict.

Regarding the Security affairs of the state, the country did tremendously improved. Ninety-nine per cent of the needed UNMIL troops were deployed in almost all parts of the country with disarmament in high gear and former combatants surrendered their weapons. With the latest report from the UNMIL information section, the disarmament estimate of combatants went above the initial estimate of sixty thousand combatants. Preparations were made for the rehabilitation and reintegration of former combatants while schools, both vocational and formal education were contracted by the UNDP and the National Commission on Disarmament, Demobilization and Reintegration (NCDDRR) for admission of former combatants into those institutions.

In addressing the National Transitional Legislative Assembly (NTLA), Chairman Bryant noted that "an educated people are a free people, and it is only through a sound educational system that citizens can make informed democratic and sound economic decisions that affect their lives." He stressed that the top priority of the NTGL was to reawaken and revitalize the educational system of the country. "Many of our youths have been denied access to education for the past 14 years because of the war and civil unrest." Because of this, the Ministry of Education and UNICEF launched the free compulsory primary education program and the Back to School program. However, the success of the program depended on the will power of the government to pay the teachers, particularly so when over 500 government school teachers from the South Eastern region of Liberia have been in Monrovia for the past two months awaiting the payment of their back pay promised them by the government.

Contrarily, while there was an outcry over suffering and economic squeeze on the downtrodden masses of the country, the government was convinced that the economy on the domestic front was gradually improving. As reported by the Minister of Finance at the time, "the performance of the revenue sector was above expectation, due mainly to the centralization of revenue collection and prudent expenditure. Total expenditure of the government amounted to US$17,521,000 and revenue collected was US$21,131,000." It was really amazing for a country that was only depending on a meager revenue collection base to make such a significant collection when all major income generating industries were all vandalized or looted in the "senseless civil war" as noted by an economist. "At least if there was electricity and water in the city they could form the bases for development even at the macro level," he added. Despite the many challenges experienced by the NTGL, coupled with apprehension by Liberians, the government was optimistic that with *an enabling security environment, and support from the international community, Liberia will overcome the challenges and once more be recognized by the comity of nations.*

Exercise: *Explain in one typed written page what you understand from the above article.*

APPENDIX 2

Article 2: Published in an Anthology of Students' Articles Journal, University of Liberia, 2012/2013
Contributed by: Richmond S. Anderson, Sr.

Title: **Who should serve as Superintendent for MCSS?**

To give a definitive yard stick for whom to serve as superintendent for the Monrovia Consolidated School System (MCSS) might be illusive, except an attempt is generated to put such a stimulating topic in perspective and relativity.

In this context, one needs to first understand certain variables about the MCSS itself, which I believe will lay an appreciable level of understanding on the subject matter.

What is the MCSS?

The MCSS is an acronym for the term Monrovia Consolidated School System, a body that provides guidance and direction for the school system in Monrovia and its environs under the Ministry of Education. This body is a government owned entity that drives the developmental agenda of the government education policy, particularly in Monrovia and its surroundings. It has authorities headed by a superintendent taken care of by government.

Who is a Superintendent?

A Superintendent is a manager, advisor or administrator that exercises control over a given local or entity. A superintendent in Liberia operates under direct instruction from the appointing powers. The superintendent of the MCSS is responsible for the supervision of the public educational system in the country's capital, Monrovia.

The MCSS was established through a charter amending the educational law in 1965 following one hundred and eighteen years of Liberia's independence. The enactment was done by the Senate and the House of Representatives of the Republic of Liberia, in Legislative Assembled.

According to Section (1) of the charter, "The Educational Law is hereby amended by adding thereto 27 new section 15 through 25-p respectively, constituting a new chapter, to be chapter 2-A". It is obvious that the establishment of the system was within the Commonwealth District of Monrovia at the time.

It can be inferred that the amendment of the educational law in 1965 could have been triggered based on the numerous challenges the educational system was faced with, especially in Monrovia at the time. The normative role expectations for MCSS superintendent have evolved over the years, incrementally becoming more extensive, complex and demanding. This I believe has engendered a stimulant for officeholders to complete a prescribed program of graduate study and subsequently head-on for the task.

Although the focus of this paper is on the MCSS superintendent, the charter placed emphasis on the council which is pivotal to conducting the affairs of the system. In section (17) of the charter, it clearly states that "There shall be created a permanent body named the Monrovia School Council which shall be responsible to the Secretary of Education (now Minister of Education), through the Under Secretary of Education (Deputy Minister) for Instruction, for the proper and efficient conduct of the Monrovia Consolidated School System, in a manner consonant with the general policies and regulations of the Department (Ministry) of Education. The Council's responsibility for the conduct of the system shall be through a City Superintendent of Schools, with staff to assist him under the direction of the Council". These symbiotic functions among the Ministry of Education, the Monrovia School Council, and the Superintendent of the MCSS with no doubt manifest a wholesome and vibrant school system in Monrovia and its environs, especially in *the establishment, refurbishment, and maintenance of schools within the system.*

In contradiction to the above expected goals, much has not been achieved over the years. Presently the MCSS is divided into three educational districts, comprising of Sinkor, Bushrod Island and Central Monrovia with a total of 28 public schools under its supervision. Looking at the population of these educational districts, particularly the young people, 28 public schools are just too minute to accommodate school going age children, no wonder why there is a mushroom of schools in almost every community in Monrovia and its suburb. The inability to establish more schools in the system (MCSS) might be appreciable, but what is more deluding is the failure to constantly maintain the very existing public schools. Few years ago, the Minister of Education was dismissed by the president of Liberia for his failure to superintend renovation work at one of the public schools in a suburb of Monrovia.

How a Superintendent is appointed?

According to the charter of the MCSS, a superintendent is appointed by the regular appointment. "The Council shall first consider names of qualified persons, and shall then submit one name to the Secretary (Minister) of Education, who shall present same to the present for approval. The president shall either confirm the appointment of the person nominated, or return the nomination to the council through the Secretary (Minister) of Education", Section 25-p. The qualification of a superintendent, according to the charter should have a minimum qualification of an earned Master's degree or earned higher degree from an accredited college or university in educational administration. The person must have five years' experience in school administration or supervision.

Responsibilities and Roles of a Superintendent

Globally, according to an astute educator Dr. Bernadeia Johnson, in her attempt to describe the responsibilities and roles of a superintendent of schools stated, "The superintendent of any school system is responsible for leading all functions and processes for the school system. The superintendent is charged with working with all internal and external stakeholders to implement and execute core strategies that produce results across the school system. The superintendent serves as the primary decision-maker and spokesperson for the school system".

By all indications, it can be construed that by provision of the charter, the superintendent is the Chief Executive Officer (CEO) of the school system. He or she sets the tone, charts the course of the system, and works closely with the school council, including the chief financial officer and the school principals. In some cases, working with the school council poses significant challenges for the superintendent. The school council is the superintendent's boss. They are responsible for hiring and firing the superintendent through the council's recommendation, and evaluating his or her performance on a regular basis.

Since it is an elected body, new members might be chosen every few years. Indisputably, this change can create a different dynamic in the relationship with the superintendent from year to year, depending on who is elected. The superintendent must also respond to the demands of all other constituencies in the school system, including the teachers, students, parents, staff and the community at large. He or she must consider how to allocate the financial and human resources of the school system in order to achieve the best results. While being mindful of all the competing demands, a great superintendent will ultimately be guided by a singular question. What is best for all students in the system?

The Responsibilities of the School Council

The charter of the MCSS highlighted several responsibilities of the school council in order to fulfill effectively its responsibilities for the proper and effective conduct of the system. Among some of the responsibilities are the holding of regular monthly meetings, nominate and employ qualified professionals and service personnel for the system, consonant with the general requirements, prepare, through the staff of the system, and operating budget, through its staff, maintain buildings and equipment of the system as well as make annual report to the Ministry of Education under the direction of the school council.

Beyond the provision in the charter, it can be emphatically averred that the school council sets the vision for the school system and the decisions they make at their monthly meetings should make a great different for the system. The word **Public** in public school refers to the fact that it is the citizens themselves who control the public schools in my belief. In some countries like the United States, school councils members are elected depending on the size and configuration of the district and most of the members must be residents of the school district.

For Liberia, particularly with the MCSS, members of the first school council following the approbation of the charter were nominated by the Minister of Education through the charter committee. Thereafter, the minster presented the committee's nomination to the president for appointment. Subsequent members of the council have been nominated by the Minister of Education for appointment by the president, according to Section (19) of the charter.

In my mind, the most important thing a school council should do is to establish a vision for the schools within the system that reflects a consensus of the council, communities and council staff. The school council has a wide variety of additional responsibilities, such as adopting a balanced annual budget and issuing interim financial reports, adopting the school calendar, negotiating contracts with employee unions, such as the MCSS Teachers Association, approving curriculum materials and closing or constructing schools.

With these varied responsibilities, educational pundits would grappled over the questions such as, what philosophy of education does the school system want the MCSS schools to have? What should the students know and be able to do when they graduate? How can schools best educate who come from diverse background? Educators believe strongly that these are some of the types of questions that a school must ponder over when trying to establish a vision.

Turning Vision into Practice

Visions are envisioned by visionaries and it is only them who can create the path for fruition. Whatever the vision may be, it's up to the superintendent to implement same. This is why one of the school's council decisions is the hiring and firing the superintendent through recommendation. It is worth noting that the school council also approves the superintendent's personnel recommendations. Since public schools are mainly for the public, school council meetings are supposed to be opened to the public with the agenda publicly posted in advance. If this is done, the public will learn a lot about the school council's policies and challenges by attending meetings. In most cases, the council meetings could be structured to the public chance to express their opinions to the school council and the community. By and large, the accomplishment of the vision of the school council squarely depends on the willingness and meticulous posture of the superintendent. The reason for this is because the superintendent must wear many hats but always keep the focus clear with the sole purpose of achieving some positive results for the system. The superintendent of the MCSS sets the direction and the tone while responding to the often competing demands on the school council, administration, teachers, parents, students and the community.

School Council and Superintendent Relationship

Even though the superintendent of the MCSS is hired by the school council through its recommendation, there must be some level of cordiality between the two, especially when it comes to the viability of the MCSS. As previously stated, the school council is responsible for setting the policies of the system, overseeing the budget and hiring and firing the superintendent. The council and the superintendent must work together to establish goals for the system, and then the superintendent must see to it that the goals and aspiration are met. In a well-run system which I believe is the case of the MCSS, the superintendent takes the broad goals set by the school council and translates them into real programs that would achieve results.

Parents and Superintendent Relationship

Though it might seem awkward and inconceivable to think that there could be a direct link with parents and the superintendent of MCSS looking at the extreme that exist, it is important to note that the same chain of command that exists in any entity is the same trend in all defined school system. For instance, if a parent's child is having a problem in his or her classroom, the parent will first communicate with the teacher. If the parent feels that the teacher is not responding adequately, he or she will contact the principal for redress. If communication fails with the principal, the parent will then take the problem to the superintendent. All these levels of seeking redress, most competent and good superintendents will want to know that the parent have attempted to handle the problem in this way before bringing it to their attention.

Indicators of an Effective and Great Superintendent

This piece of writing is in no way trying to create a benchmark or yard stick to measure the qualities of a superintendent operating or to operate in a system, but rather an attempt to share personal experience gained over the years as an instructor, administrator, educator, government official and politician. Against this backdrop, an American life-long Democrat Howard Schultz one time addressing a cross section of people said "I am convinced that most people can achieve their dreams and beyond if they have the determination to keep trying", hence any superintendent of the MCSS who must be acclaimed by the public should to some degree possess these qualities. With this premise therefore, the expected qualities of any great superintendent of the system must have a clear vision for the system instead of being title guided by the power that be. The superintendent must have the zest to work with school system to set the vision, goals and objectives of the system, and exert all efforts to make sure that the goals are achieved.

Since a superintendent is head of school system, he or she must be an instructional leader. The superintendent must know that the most pivotal role of the school system is making sure students are learning and achieving at high levels academically. He or she must be knowledgeable of the best practices for maximizing students' achievements and is supportive of teachers in the school system.

Beyond any reasonable doubt, a great superintendent should be an effective communicator regardless of his or her academic achievement. He or she must make a concerted effort to communicate the needs, aspirations and accomplishments of the school system in a variety formats through comprehensive written reports, communication with the media, public meetings and attendance of school events within the school system.

The world over, management is the propelling wheel that promotes efficiency, viability and sustenance in any given or established organization. In this light, a superintendent of the MCSS must be a good manager. He or she should be able to direct the administrators to accomplish the goals of the school system, monitor on a regular basis the administrators' progress and evaluate their performance.

Another cardinal indicator that enhances congenial and mutual working relationship in entities that fosters productivity is the ability to be a good listener. As a superintendent of the school system leading thousands of people form diverse cultural background, you are a leader. Therefore, you must be a good listener to understand the issues and concerns of the people you are leading to enable you make the best decision.

As a global phenomenon, most heads of both private and public institutions do not venture in risk taking. They are of the pessimist that taking risk will be to the detriment of the organization and this could lead to their failure. But as a leader risk taking is one of the potentials that make you great depending on the management of risk. For a superintendent of MCSS, he or she must not be afraid to take risk or make a commitment. An average superintendent might set goals that are either vague or easily achieved but a great superintendent would not be afraid to boldly set goals, such as "Most of the second graders will be able to read by the end of the school year," and then put the programs and resources in place to achieve those goals.

One of the indicators that most leaders many a time overlook is flexibility. Due to this insensitivity to flexibility many organizations end up collapsing as the regimental posture displayed by most leader leaders. As leader, particularly in the MCSS one should be flexible. He or she needs to be able to manage the politics of the job to adapt to new school council members, changes in the system funding and changes in the school community while not sacrificing the system's vision. A great superintendent should take a collaborative approach rather than a confrontational approach in dealing with issues at all levels in the community and system.

Challenges in the MCSS

There is no system globally that is void of challenges, no matter how good it might appear. In a holistic manner, as this paper has endeavored to look at the generic ingredients of **who should be a superintendent for MCSS**, it is also wanting to focus on some challenges that may have faced the entity over the years, especially during post war Liberia. Currently, the public school system in Monrovia is not at its best. However, there is some level of progress amidst the difficulties faced by the public schools in Monrovia due to financial strangulations, not only for the system but the country as hole.

To give a retrospective look at things following the cessation of hostilities in Liberia, particularly in Monrovia and its environs following the signing of the **Accra Comprehensive Agreement (CPA)** in 2003 in Accra, Ghana by parties to the conflict, a National Transitional Government was put in place headed by His Excellency C. Guyde Bryant. Chairman Bryant led Transitional Government was faced with enormous challenges since in fact the country's (Liberia) economy was in complete shambles. Every facet of the country's strata, including schools, was gravely affected.

As this trend of financial degradation permeated the country, the transitional government could not cope to maintain public schools in Monrovia and its surroundings. This situation got manifested in 2004 when thousands of public school students from the Monrovia Consolidated Scholl System (MCSS), during the early morning hours of Friday, April 2nd, went on the violent and unstoppable rampage in Monrovia and its environs, thereby disrupting normal businesses. The angry students threw stones and other harmful objects at the Ministry of Finance and Education, as they continued their protest.

Due to the students' violent protest, employees of the two ministries who showed up for work on that Friday morning locked themselves up in the buildings, while others fled as the students remained uncompromising with their action. Even some journalists who went on the scene to cover the event were attacked by some of the students upon observing that the journalists were doing photo coverage of the protest. "I managed to have escape from the mob action but all of my equipment, including my digital camera, tape recorder, and personal cash were taken away by some angry students", was the sorrowful saying by reporter J. Josephus Gray of the Perspective Newspaper.

Some of the students were seem chasing vehicles while some sat in the middle of Broad Street in front of both Education and Finance Ministries. They vowed against leaving until their instructors' demands were addressed. Besides, other students from the William V. S. Tubman High School stormed a nearby run United Methodist School – Joseph Jenkins Roberts High School and beat up some of their colleagues mercilessly who apparently refused to have joined them in the protest action.

However, as the protest action of the disgruntled students became intensive and unbearable, personnel of the United Nations Mission in Liberia, (UNMIL) that is the military component, in collaboration with personnel of the Liberia National Police (LNP) managed to quell the situation but the gravity and extent of destruction encountered remained unknown.

During the protest, the total number of students arrested and detained was not known. More importantly, there was no report of death or looting which are often characterized by numerous protests such as the 1979 rice riot, which brought the country to collapse. As the students raged, several other persons, especially workers fled from their private offices to seek refuge at the diplomatic enclave of Mamba Point, near the United States Embassy.

As the students quest for financial compensation for teachers gained momentum, public school teachers following a week of the protest, abandoned classes in demand of their salary arrears and other benefits. The teachers' action negatively affected the students since it denied of sitting the semester examinations, while their colleagues from private and mission schools were attending unhampered and interruptive. The precarious financial situation that permeated the Liberian society during the Chairman Bryant NTGL was an inheritance from the Taylor led government. The deposed regime of exiled former leader, President Charles G. Taylor was indebted to civil servants including public school teachers over 12 months' salary arrears, something the nation's work-force wanted the transitional government settle expeditiously.

In an attempt to get out of this financial quark mire, the MCSS in 2012 appealed to the president of Liberia seeking autonomy status of the system. Making the appeal on behalf of the system at the William V. S. Tubman High School during a brief visitation by President Ellen Johnson-Sirleaf, the President of the Monrovia Consolidated School System Principal Association, Daniel Mulbah informed the president that the MCSS is faced with many challenges that they could solve independently, but have to wait on government's intervention for solution since the system is under the supervision of the Liberian government.

What he did say however according to my recollection, is how the system intends to generate funds to operate those schools being supported *by the government as well as pay salaries for instructors and staff of the school system. Following the appeal to President Sirleaf, there were growing apprehensions that if the system obtained autonomy parents of children may be asked to pay tuition and other fees, including chairs and instructional materials being provided by the state, which could undermine government's free primary education program.*

In defending his appeal for autonomy, Mr. Mulbah noted that if the appeal was considered, the MCSS needs to have its "own teeth to bite" and solve some those problems of over crowdedness of schools, building of more schools, and building the capacity of MCSS members, constant periodic maintenance of school buildings amongst others.

With determination in his appeal, Mr. Mulbah urged the President to take seriously the plight of teachers in the employ of the MCSS, while stressing the need for the construction of more schools in Montserrado County to accommodate students desirous of enrolling in its institution. He further appealed to the Liberian leader to address the problem of transportation and allowances, something he said are impeding the smooth operation of the entity.

Apart from the above stated challenges faced the MCSS, there are other numerous challenges that are contributive factors that tend to erode the effective functioning of the MCSS. Some of the reasons responsible for the difficulties experienced by the public school system in Monrovia include incompetence, lack of commitment, corruption, eye service among others. Despite of these difficulties, the government schooling system in the capital has enjoyed some progress and advantages also. Some of them are better paying structure, proper representation, quality output, and capacity building.

Just as the physical and social development of the average child's is beset with many problems, so also is the development of education in any society is hampered by a variety of problems, some of which are associated with the responsibility for and control of the society education. This situation has the propensity to retard the pace of the educational development of the school system. In view of the aforementioned, as we strive in understanding who should serve superintendent of the MCSS, it is important that we take a keen look individually at some of the difficulties and advantages faced the system as listed below.

Incompetence

Incompetence is a term that refers to the lack of ability or lack of skill on the part of an individual to perform well in certain task assigned thus leading to the downward growth of the institution that is entrusted someone with such responsibility. In the case of the MCSS, there has been point in time where superintendents who are incompetent are being appointed to carry the system forward. Some of the reasons why there are incompetent superintendents taken over the Monrovia Consolidated School System include lack of qualification or nepotism at the as compared these days where you see more quest for higher qualification. Due to the incompetence of some of these superintendents, the MCSS has falter on its responsibilities thereby bringing the educational system below standard. Given their incompetence, the MCSS had struggled to grapple with current day reality.

Lack of Commitment

Another factor responsible for the devastating blow experienced by the MCSS is the issue of lack of commitment. The issue of lack of commitment has not only affected the MCSS alone, but almost all of our various sectors in the country. The term, lack of commitment refers to the "don't care" attitude of some public officials who are given task to perform but accept the challenge only for the benefit of the cash and not the service or the output of the portfolio given. With this attitude, they put they put up a lackadaisical attitude not wanting to know whether their lieutenants are up to the task or the goals targeted are been achieved.

Corruption

Apart from the above problems haunting the school system in Monrovia, the endemic and cancerous societal ill is not left out of the woes of the school system. Corruption is a deadly weapon that needs to be destroyed and weeded out of the system. Corruption has caused most of the superintendent to head the school system ineffective. Some of the superintendents, when employed, take up the notion of using the position to enrich themselves, legally or illegally. They will, out of selfish desire convert the materials and logistics intended for the development of the system to their personal use thereby crippling the operation of the educational system. As evidenced in a chart with one of the principals of an MCSS school in the Monrovia area, "since we were instructed by the Ministry of Education to collect our school's supplies from our District Educational Officer, it is almost two months I have not seen him or receive the supplies". When such a situation takes place, the end result is the low productivity coming out of the system, the under performance of the students, the misrepresentation of the educational sector and chattered national educational system.

Eye Service

Another trouble eating up the educational fabric of the Monrovia Consolidated School is the issue of eye service. When it appears that the higher authority to the superintendent is passionate about the system and will do anything to get the system progressing, he or she valuing the money than the work will play a game called eye service. Eye service is where someone delegated with a responsibility will act to be performing the assigned responsibility when the overall authority is around, when in reality the work is not been done. When eye servicing is carried out, the system is stagnated and will only move forward when the questioning authority comes around.

Inadequate Classroom Accommodation

Most schools within the school system of the MCSS, classroom accommodation is grossly inadequate. As a result of the large enrolment, the classrooms are usually overcrowded, with up to seventy or more students receiving instructions in classrooms designed for only thirty or, thirty-five students in line with international standard. In most cases, the chairs and desks are not enough for the students. If one were to go on a visitation to public schools within the school system, you will observe students sitting on one arm chair, standing up, or sitting to the window of the classroom. When classrooms are crowded with students in such a manner, there is a stalling of teaching-learning process and a disruption of the students' mental activity, a situation that generally militates against effective learning and intellectual development of the students.

Poorly Equipped Libraries, Laboratories and Subject Rooms

For effective teaching and learning, well equipped libraries, laboratories and subject rooms are needed, but the truth of the matter is that, major schools in the school system presently lack these essential facilities. It is no doubt that, many of the schools have buildings or provision on their campuses they call libraries, but most of them are not equipped with the needed books and current journals or magazines that would enhance the learning quest of students. Also, most schools in the system do not have science laboratories while the few schools that have do not possess the basic tools or equipment such as microscope, dissecting instruments and specimens.

Also, many schools within the MCSS do not have special rooms for teaching basic subjects such as history, geography, and French. In such a situation, the teachers cannot put in their best, and the students too cannot drive maximum benefit from the instruction being given. Again, the teaching-learning process is stalled and overall development of the children, within the school system is retarded.

Unstable Teachers

As far teaching staff in the school system today is concern, the problem is on longer that of unavailability of teachers, but rather that of instability. This does not help the development of the educational system. Due to the comparative poorer conditions of services of teachers in the school system, the tendency for most teachers today, as was the case during the 1980s, is to use the teaching profession as stepping stone to higher esteemed and more attractive jobs.

In consequence of this, teaching is gradually becoming a profession for fresh graduates of universities and colleges in education who are ready to call it a quit, without provocation, as soon as they find greener pastures. From time to time, therefore, the teaching in the school system is usually becoming unstable, as averred by a teacher in one of the schools in the school system, "my friend, I am not kidding I have too much burden, teaching in one school will not help me, I have to do moon lighting, that is teaching from school to school". The consequence for this is the stalling of the teaching-learning process, with the students being greatly affected. "Unless the conditions of service of teachers, at all levels, are improved *and their status rose higher in the school system, the teaching staff of educational institutions shall continue to be unstable and educational progress shall continue to be retarded", the teacher added.*

Conclusion

Despite these insurmountable challenges, the school system for the past few years has experienced some considerable level of progress in its postwar status. Such progress seen in recent times is better pay structure for teachers which have been one of the constant problems affecting the system in time past. Furthermore, most of the instructional personnel in the school system are either qualified or are academically sojourning for better and advanced qualification both at home and abroad. Since the incumbency of President Ellen Johnson-Sirleaf in 2006, both graduate schools in educational administration and supervision at the University of Liberia and the Cutington University continue to graduate more students in educational programs and subsequently assigned to various private and public schools. Having dissected the treats and virtues of a superintendent in any given school system, it will be obvious that who should be a superintendent of the MCSS should be one who must fulfill the indicators listed in the above notation.

This, I strongly believe would facilitate efficiency and maximum productivity for the school system.

THE ABOVE ARTICLE CAN BE PLACED IN CONTEXT TO ANY SCHOOL SYSTEM IN AFRICA OR BEYOND. EDUCATION IS DYNAMIC AND UNIVERSAL.

Exercise: **In one paragraph, summarize the above article according to your understanding, and do a comparative analysis of the two articles.**

APPENDIX 3

Editorial #1. Published by THE CHRONICLE Newspaper of Ghana
Vol.27 No. 72, Friday 27th April 2018

Editorial Title: Police transformation agenda is on course

The full content as published

The Ghana Police Service exists to deliver services in crime prevention and detection, apprehension and prosecution of offenders, consistent with the expectations of Ghanaians. Community Policing is an emerging concept in policing which seeks to help bridge the communication and interaction gap between police institutions and the communities they serve.

*In the 23rd April 2018 edition of **The Chronicle,** we reported on the development of hundreds of uniformed police personnel on the streets of Accra to tackle the recent upsurge in armed robbery in the national capital. The development forms part of the transformation programmer launched by the IGP, David Asante Apeatu, at the beginning of the year, which seeks to make the Ghana Police Service a world class one. **The Chronicle** has witnessed the massive deployment of police officers at strategic locations in Accra to stop and search vehicles at random.*

In addition to the above, the latest police response to the increase in robberies committed by motorcyclists has seen the launch of a new specialized unit, whose members have been trained in high-risk crime prevention tactics. The specially-trained unit, made up of 70 police officers, has been operating in some communities in Accra to ensure safer neighborhoods, and plans are ongoing to extend this crime-prevention initiative to other parts of the country. Since his appointment, the Inspector General of Police has indeed, been on a serious campaign to clamp down on the activities of criminals. According to IGP David Asante-Apeatu: "The police no longer sits and wait for crime to be reported for action to be taken, neither does it rely on the traditional crime prevention and detection methodologies," This shows that the police are now up and doing and are ready to carry the fight to the criminals.

He also sounded a word of caution to those who use motorbikes to commit crimes, saying the launch of the new specialized unit will also help in combating robberies committed by motorcyclists. Much as The Chronicle is saluting the Ghana Police Service for a good job done so far, we also want to caution about the few bad nuts in the service, which could drag their image into disrepute. The police should be welcoming to the general public who report issues of the police corruption and indiscipline. When reports concerning police misconducts are made to the Police Intelligence and Professional Standards (PIPS) for disciplinary action to be taken, justice must be seen to be done. This way, the confidence the public has in the Police Service will be enhanced. The service should, therefore, be very concerned about its image and be ready to deal with officers who misconduct themselves.

We wish the Ghana Police Service the best of luck as it strives to actualize its vision of becoming a world-class police service.

DID YOU NOTICE ANYTHING IN THE ARTICLE FROM YOUR READING OF THE BOOK CONCERNING EDITORIAL WRITING? *Explore and make an attempt to write one editorial on any contemporary issue.*

APPENDIX 4

**Editorial #: 2 Published by THE PUBLISHER Newspaper of Ghana
No. 043/18 Monday 16th – Tuesday, 17th April 2018
Editorial Title: The Looming Crisis of Unemployed Youth**

The full content as published

All is still not well for the several thousands of Ghanaian youth that remain unemployed or under employed with no clear hope of a good job anywhere anytime soon. The growing army of unemployed youth is frightening. Sadly, the constituency includes well educated young persons including graduates that still cannot find jobs, despite their university qualification.

It is even frightening that a huge number of the unemployed youth are simply unemployable. They are neither lettered nor skilled. They have not learnt any trade or vocation. They have no certificates or academic qualification.

The danger is that they are able bodied young adults with a lot of energy and hot adrenalin running through their veins. Thousands of able bodied adults that are both idle and frustrated. That is where the danger lies. An energized, anger and frustrated youth….hundreds of thousands of them.

The issue of joblessness and or unemployment for that matter, is one crisis

THE PUBLISHER is surprised has still not been declared a national emergency. It is not only the unemployed youth that suffers from the effects of unemployment. It has a direct negative impact on the country's economy and growth. When the young adults have a challenge in finding jobs, it simply means they take longer times to get married, settle down and become happy workers paying their taxes. We all had a shocking reminder of this joblessness when over 84,0000 young persons turned up for a recruitment exercise that was expecting just some 500 people.

And that was just for the Ghana Immigration Services (GIS). Similar or even larger numbers are expected to show up when the Police Service, the Fire Service or the Army announce recruitment exercises. The National Youth Employment Policy (NYPA), an initiative of former President John Kufor, was able to mitigate the crisis but has proven not to be an effective or lasting solution. Clearly, there is a defect with our educational curriculum that trains people to graduate and start to look for nonexistent jobs instead of training people to come out of school with the training to establish jobs themselves. For decades, our educational module has proven to be defective yet we continue to use the same strategy and expect to get a different answer. We are sick.

We the introduction of the free Senior High School policy, it is expected that enrolment in school would go up but as a country, we have not planned on what to do with the products that would be coming out of the schools.

Of course, if nothing is done with a sense of urgency, they would come out of school only to add to the already alarming number of unemployed youth. Certainly, we need to start thinking right and start thinking now.

APPENDIX 5

Editorial #:3 Published by THE INQUIRER Newspaper of Liberia
Vol. 18 No. 4 Tuesday, January 20, 2009
Editorial Title: Armed Robbery, No Solution?

The full content as published

FOR THE PAST few weeks, we have observed that armed robbery has begun creeping once again in the city of Monrovia and its surroundings, with many residents falling prey to the act. According to latest cases that have been reported, armed robbery activities occur at least once or twice in most communities in the past four weeks with most residents victimized.

THE LATEST OF these incidents occurred in the Jamaica Road, Slipway, Doe Community and now the Old Road areas, where it has been gathered that the assailants stormed the premises of the victims and made away with huge amount of money and other valuables. The robbers inflicted serious body injuries on some of the victims in the execution of their of their devilish act, and as part of its efforts to deal with the situation, the Liberia National Police (LNP) last week, publicly announced that it has rounded up eight alleged robbers in a police operation and that it was on the hunt for several others.

WHILE WELCOMING THE move to train the Emergency Response Unit (ERU), of the LNP, in dealing with cases such as armed robbery, which is a significant boost in the fight against crimes such as armed robbery, we think there is still much to be done to ensure that the residents across the country live in a secured environment.

FROM WHAT WE have seen thus far, such as the arrest of some of the alleged perpetrators and the response of the police to some of these incidents, we think the efforts to deal with the issue is well on course but the police needs to redouble its efforts and do away with complacency in tackling the issue. By this we mean the police should increase its night patrols and put in place extra security measures that would help deal with the situation.

IT IS OUR plea that the police should strive to work and make its communication system more efficient by making sure that the available numbers to the public are pro-active to the extent that when there is an emergency, residents would be able to ring the police immediately. This plea comes against the backdrop that so many people are complaining that they do not get through any of the numbers assigned to the police, thus making it very difficult for the force to come to their rescue.

ONCE AGAIN, WE call on the LNP to redouble its efforts in dealing with the problem of armed robbery by increasing its night patrols and overhaul the communication system in a way that it would be highly responsive to the call of the people when they are unfolding incidents of robbery.

GENERAL QUESTIONS

1. Why do you need to understand the word perspective?
2. According to your reading or understanding, what is perspective?
3. What is the difference between opinion writing and research writing?
4. What do you mean by etymology?
5. What is content knowledge?
6. What does analytical writing do to your writing ability?
7. Name and explain the four types of analytical writing.
8. What is the primary purpose of descriptive writing?
9. What is analytical writing?
10. What is critical writing?
11. What does analytical framework entails?
12. What is feature?
13. Unlike the straightforward news, feature article goes beyond just the mere facts. Discuss.
14. What is your understanding on "feature versus an opinion" and "feature versus a news report"?
15. What makes the writing style of a news story and that of a feature different?
16. In conventional writing (news), what two things do you two things do you consider?
17. Most often, feature stories are framed by the specific experiences of those who drive the news or those who are affected by it. Explain.
18. What are the characteristics in journalistic or feature writing?
19. State and explain with examples the various types of feature.
20. What makes the elements of feature important?

21. What is your take on the "SPE Anderson Theory of Communication"?
22. List at least six characteristics of a feature.
23. enumerate and explain five qualities of a feature.
24. Why is the usage of simple diction or words important in journalistic writing?
25. Just as in the normal essay writing, feature writing is of no exception in its package. Why?
26. What are some of the things to consider when writing a feature piece?
27. Prewriting your feature article entails what?
28. The lead, or introduction of a feature must catch the reader's attention and make him or her want to read more. Use any attention-getting device suitable to your topic. Make sure, too, that the lead sets the tone for the article. Examples of leads are...
29. Explain "there is greater freedom in feature writing"
30. Name five key tips in writing a good feature piece.
31. What are those things to remember when writing a feature article?
32. Overall, feature articles use an informative tone while incorporating creative and descriptive devices in order to increase audience taste or appeal. Explain.
33. Who is a feature writer?
34. As a beginner of feature writing, name five tips mostly needed.
35. A strong lead paragraph offers intrigue from the start. Editors don't have time to read through the entire article to research your key point, and neither do your readers. Explain.
36. What do you know about feature leads?
37. A quote can lend authority to an article, introduce an expert and further advance the story. Explain.
38. What is your understanding on "consequences of reporting feature article"?
39. Explain "facts versus truth in feature writing"
40. What do you mean by fairness in feature writing?
41. Explain the ethical aspect in feature writing.
42. Editorial, in the real sense or by way of definition, is the unified or corporate voice or stand of any operative media institution on any given issue affecting the interest of the public. Explain.

43. Explain "editorial versus news writing and editorial versus feature".
44. List and explain five hints to write a good editorial.
45. List and discuss the various types of editorials.
46. Explain the distinctive nature of an editorial and enumerate the qualities of a good editorial.
47. Discuss the features of an editorial and relate your discussion to the nature of editorial.
48. Enumerate and discuss the various types of editorial audience.
49. In writing an editorial, where do you source your materials or data?
50. Discuss the techniques involved in writing an editorial.
51. Discuss the qualities of a good editorial writer.
52. Discuss the functions the editorial board.
53. Explain the desirability and inevitability of editorials in newspapers.
54. Discuss the relevance of research in editorial writing.
55. Explain the relationship between research and editorial.
56. Define and outline the importance of public opinion.
57. Discuss the structure of public opinion.
58. What do you mean by "editorial versus public opinion?
59. Discuss the commonality between opinion and editorials
60. Define and discuss in detail persuasion and editorial writing
61. Discuss some tips in persuasive writing
62. Why are persuasive techniques necessary in editorial writing?
63. Outline any ten propaganda techniques you know and discuss four of them.
64. Persuasion and propaganda techniques are pivotal in editorial writing. Why?
65. Discuss all you know about public perception on propaganda
66. Why is propaganda important in editorial writing?
67. On a broader basis, discus ethical issues as it relates to editorial writing
68. What do you mean by "advocacy journalism"?
69. Receiving bribes and brown envelopes are unethical in the profession. Discuss.
70. Every media institution must be guided by ethics or code of conduct. List any four of what you know regarding ethics or code of conduct and discuss.

71. Why is editorial important for stakeholders of national political actors?
72. Discuss the relevance of editorial in national development.
73. Write at least ten paragraphs on each of the below listed:

    a. Personality profile feature
    b. Human interest feature
    c. Historical feature
    d. Seasonal feature

74. Identify contemporary issues in your country in the areas of education, health, agriculture, commerce, social and students' politics on campus and contact stakeholders where to collect your data as sources and write 20 (twenty) paragraphs of appreciable and publishable feature articles on each of the above listed issues.
75. Look around your campus, your community, read newspapers or monitor the radio, use your mass communication or journalism traits by using your intuition to smell or hear the news and write editorials on those occurrences, especially those that have impact on society.

Printed in the United States
by Baker & Taylor Publisher Services